AA

50 Walks in
ESSEX

D0348377

First published 2002
Researched and written by Katerina and Eric Roberts

Produced by AA Publishing
© Automobile Association Developments Limited 2002
Illustrations © Automobile Association Developments Limited 2002

Published by AA Publishing (a trading name of Automobile
Association Developments Limited, whose registered office is
Millstream, Maidenhead, Windsor, SL4 5GD;
registered number 1878835). A00905

ISBN 0 7495 3332 3

A CIP catalogue record for this book is available
from the British Library.

The contents of this book are believed correct at the time of printing.
Nevertheless, the publishers cannot be held responsible for any errors
or omissions or for changes in the details given in this book or for
the consequences of any reliance on the information it provides. We
have tried to ensure accuracy in this book, but things do change and
we would be grateful if readers would advise us of any inaccuracies
they may encounter.

We have taken all reasonable steps to ensure that these walks are
safe and achievable by walkers with a realistic level of fitness.
However, all outdoor activities involve a degree of risk and the
publishers accept no responsibility for any injuries caused to
readers whilst following these walks. For more advice on walking
safely see page 128. The mileage range shown on the front cover is for
guidance only – some walks may exceed or be less than these
distances.

Visit the AA Publishing website at www.theAA.com

Paste-up and editorial by Outcrop Publishing Services Ltd, Cumbria
for AA Publishing

Colour reproduction by LC Repro
Printed in Italy by G Canale & C SPA, Torino, Italy

Legend

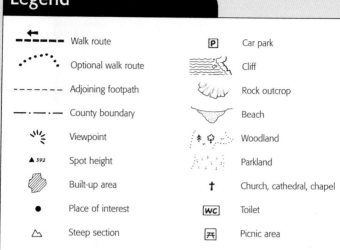

← ▬▬▬▬	Walk route	P	Car park
••••••••	Optional walk route	≈≈≈	Cliff
▬ ▬ ▬ ▬	Adjoining footpath		Rock outcrop
▬•▬•▬•	County boundary		Beach
☼	Viewpoint		Woodland
▲392	Spot height		Parkland
▨	Built-up area	†	Church, cathedral, chapel
●	Place of interest	WC	Toilet
△	Steep section	⊼	Picnic area

Essex locator map

Contents

Contents

	WALK	RATING	DISTANCE	PAGE	
27	A Castle at Pleshey	●○○	3 miles (4.8km)	71	E183
28	The Longer Ongar walk	●●○	6½ miles (10.4km)	74	E183
29	Cold War Kelvedon Hatch	●●○	9¾ miles (15.7km)	77	
30	Bringing Home the Bacon at Little Dunmow	●●○	4 miles (6.4km)	78	E195
31	Brawling and Benefactors Around Great Bardfield	●○○	4½ miles (7.2km)	80	E195
32	The Sound of Music at Thaxted	●○○	3 miles (4.8km)	83	E195
33	From Saffron Walden	●●○	5½ miles (8.8km)	86	E195
34	Around Audley End	●○○	3 miles (4.8km)	89	
35	Saffron Walden Town	●○○	3½ miles (5.7km)	90	E195
36	Lambourne End to Chigwell	●●●	9 miles (14.5km)	92	E174
37	Old and New Come Together at Harlow	●○○	4 miles (6.4km)	95	E174
38	Matching the Villages	●○○	3½ miles (5.7km)	98	E183
39	A Hike to Hatfield Heath	●●○	6 miles (9.7km)	101	
40	Hatfield Forest	●○○	4½ miles (7.2km)	102	E195
41	Pretty Ugley	●○○	5½ miles (8.8km)	104	E195
42	Taking Off from Stansted	●○○	3¼ miles (5.3km)	107	E195
43	On the Ground at Stansted	●●○	5¾ miles (9.2km)	110	E195
44	Stansted Mountfitchet	●●○	4¾ miles (7.7km)	113	
45	A Roam Around Roding Valley Nature Reserve	●○○	3 miles (4.8km)	114	E174
46	Epping Forest Retreat	●●○	7¼ miles (11.7km)	116	E174
47	A Scout Round Gilwell Park	●●●	6 miles (9.7km)	119	E174
48	Lee Valley Park	●●●	7½ miles (12.1km)	122	E174
49	Waltham Abbey	●●●	9 miles (14.5km)	125	
50	Theydon Bois to the End of the Line	●●○	4 miles (6.4km)	126	E174

Rating: Each walk is rated for its relative difficulty compared to the other walks in this book. Walks marked ●○○ are likely to be shorter and easier with little total ascent. The hardest walks are marked ●●●.

Walking in Safety: For advice and safety tips ► 128.

Introducing Essex

Let's explode a few myths. Essex is not flat, Essex Man does not drive like the clappers in a white van and only some Essex girls wear white court shoes and dance around their handbags! If you climb up the Langdon Hills, explore the Lee Valley, wander along the high ridges of Hainault Forest or trek up Halstead's High Street, you will discover that Essex is far from being a featureless and uninteresting county.

It is true, however, that Essex has neither the hills or dales of Yorkshire nor the mountain ranges of Wales or the Highlands of Scotland, but this county has plenty of other attractions, many of which can only be appreciated by walking. Take for instance London's dramatic urban skyline punctuated by the capital's tallest building, Canary Wharf, which on a clear day is visible from as far away as Danbury and Basildon, or surreal views of the busy M25 from places around London's third airport at Stansted.

Old rivers with their tidal estuaries were the routes which the first invaders took as they sailed from the North Sea into what became known as the country of the East Saxons. They established settlements, which in turn attracted trade; waterways were built to transport goods to London and throughout the centuries European settlers arrived and contributed to the social and cultural landscape of this fascinating county.

Walking a little off the beaten track will lead you to the rural retreats of deepest Essex where agriculture survives alongside new housing estates and old villages, often devoid of people during the day, as they travel to Colchester and Chelmsford for work. But in many parts, agriculture still plays an important role, as does tourism in pleasant little towns, such as Stansted Mountfitchet and Saffron Walden and seaside resorts like Walton-on-the-Naze.

The majority of the walks in this book are circular and vary in length from 2 miles (3.2km) to 10 miles (16.1km). They are mainly rural and coastal walks, with welcoming pubs not too far away. One walk, from Theydon Bois to Epping, is linear and easily accessible via London Underground's Central Line. The Essex landscape is indeed varied, from the high land in the north and west, where the views from Langdon Hills should not be missed, to the flat coastal plains of the Dengie Peninsular, which have a certain raw beauty best appreciated on a cold, windswept day. Also included is a maritime stroll around Harwich and two city walks; one in

PUBLIC TRANSPORT ⓘ

For train times call anytime on 08457 48 49 50. For services between Fenchurch Street Station and Southend (Walks 21, 23, 24, 25) call 08457 67 87 65. For information on services between Liverpool Street Station and Colchester (Walks 1, 2, 3, 4, 5, 11, 15, 20) Liverpool Street and Cambridge (Walks 33, 34, 35, 37, 42, 43) and Liverpool Street and Chingford (Walk 46) call 08459 50 50 50. For Walks 45, 50, London Underground information is available on 0207 222 1234.
Information on bus times and routes is available daily from 7AM to 11PM on 0870 608 2608.

the footsteps of Romans in Britain's oldest recorded town, Colchester, and the other around the historic sights of the county town of Chelmsford. And for relative easy walking, there are several country parks offering well-maintained footpaths and superb recreational and educational facilities.

Some of the walks included in this collection, such as the ones in Epping Forest and near Stansted's runway, are easily accessible from London's Liverpool Street Station, but for sheer isolation and a chance to discover yourself, don't overlook the invigorating coastal walks described at Paglesham Creek, Rochford, Bradwell-on-Sea and Tilbury.

Finally, we should point out that these walks have been tried and tested by a real Essex girl, Sadie, an 11-year old boxer rottweiler cross for whom we occasionally dog-sit and often dog-walk in the absence of her owners. Sadie has a mind of her own, and at her age, a discerning nose for canine-friendly excursions. We hope that her comments prove helpful for those wishing to walk their own four-legged pals in Essex.

Using this Book

Information panels

An information panel for each walk shows its relative difficulty (➤ 5), the distance and total amount of ascent. An indication of the gradients you will encounter is shown by the rating ▲▲ ▲▲ ▲▲ (no steep slopes) to ▲▲ ▲▲ ▲▲ (several very steep slopes).

Maps

There are 30 maps, covering 40 of the walks. Some walks have a suggested option in the same area. The information panel for these walks will tell you how much extra walking is involved. On short-cut suggestions the panel will tell you the total distance if you set out from the start of the main walk. Where an option returns to the same point on the main walk, just the distance of the loop is given. Where an option leaves the main walk at one point and returns to it at another, then the distance shown is for the whole walk. The minimum time suggested is for reasonably fit walkers and doesn't allow for stops. Each walk has a suggested map. Laminated aqua3 maps are longer lasting and water resistant.

Start Points

The start of each walk is given as a six-figure grid reference prefixed by two letters indicating which 100km square of the National Grid it refers to. You'll find more information on grid references on most Ordnance Survey maps.

Dogs

We have tried to give dog owners useful advice about how dog friendly each walk is. Please respect other countryside users. Keep your dog under control, especially around livestock, and obey local bylaws and other dog control notices.

Car Parking

Many of the car parks suggested are public, but occasionally you may find you have to park on the roadside or in a lay-by. Please be considerate when you leave your car, ensuring that access roads or gates are not blocked and that other vehicles can pass safely.

Walk 1

Harwich's Seafarers and Wanderers

An easy town walk discovering Harwich's exciting maritime past.

•DISTANCE•	4 miles (6.4km)
•MINIMUM TIME•	1hr 30min
•ASCENT / GRADIENT•	Negligible
•LEVEL OF DIFFICULTY•	
•PATHS•	Town streets and promenade with gentle cliffs
•LANDSCAPE•	Coast, beach, cliffs and town
•SUGGESTED MAP•	aqua3 OS Explorer 197 Ipswich, Felixstowe & Harwich
•START / FINISH•	Grid reference: TM 259328
•DOG FRIENDLINESS•	Between 1 May and 30 September dogs have to be on lead on promenade and cliff walks
•PARKING•	Free car parks at Ha'penny Pier and informal street parking
•PUBLIC TOILETS•	Beside Quayside House opposite Ha'penny Pier

BACKGROUND TO THE WALK

One of the main gateways to the Continent, Harwich is a must for *aficionados* of all things maritime. The town lies beside the grey North Sea on an isthmus between Dovercourt and Bathside bays, overlooking the Stour and Orwell estuaries and drew not only invaders and traders to its shores but adventurers and explorers too. In the 12th century a violent storm caused the rivers to break their banks and form the promontory where Harwich stands today. Realising its strategic importance the lord of the manor developed the site into a walled town. You can see the remains of his wall in St Nicholas' churchyard.

The walk begins at the Ha'penny Pier where you can spot ferries sailing to and from Europe, against a backdrop of giraffe-like cranes rising from the flat Felixstowe coast. Keeping the sea to your left you'll see traditional inns, such as the Globe, in Kings Quay Street. Such pubs were once stormed by press gangs who kidnapped boys for service in the Royal Navy. Trying to escape forceable enlistment, hapless lads would scurry like rats into the labyrinthine passages linking the houses, but many were caught and never seen again.

Famous Visitors

The town has played host to some famous faces too. Sir Francis Drake dropped in on his way to Spain and Queen Elizabeth I stayed here, remarking that 'It is a pretty town that wants for nothing'. Diarist Samuel Pepys was the local MP and Lord Nelson sojourned here with Lady Hamilton. Home-grown boys include Christopher Jones, captain of the *Mayflower*, the ship in which the Pilgrim Fathers sailed from Plymouth to the Americas in 1620.

Wander at will and see the quirky, two-wheel man operated treadwheel crane on Harwich Green or climb the Redoubt, built to fend off a threatened Napoleonic invasion, for great sea views. Along the seafront is a pair of 19th-century lighthouses. The first is the Low Lighthouse, now the Maritime Museum and the other, just 150yds (137m) inland, is the High Lighthouse. They were built by General Rebow, a get-rich-quick entrepreneur who charged each ship a penny per ton to come into port. When Rebow got wind that the

Walk 1

sandbanks were shifting he craftily sold the lighthouses to Trinity House. On the way to Dovercourt you'll pass Beacon Hill Fort, dating back to Roman times, although the gun emplacements here are of World War One and World War Two vintage. As you round the breakwater there are fine beaches and another pair of cast iron lighthouses mounted on stilts, built to replace the earlier ones at Harwich. They, too, became redundant (in 1917) but serve as yet another reminder of Harwich's seafaring history.

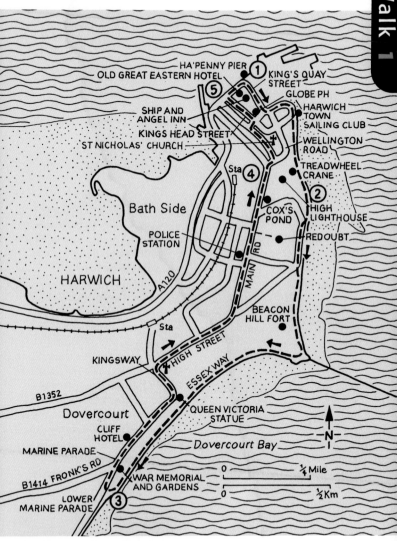

Walk 1 Directions

① With your back to **Ha'penny Pier** turn left along **The Quay** and follow the road into **Kings Quay**

Street. Turn left just before the colourful mural, painted by the Harwich Society and Harwich School in 1982 and again in 1995, which depicts local buildings and ships. Follow the road, with the sea on your left, until it turns inland. Take the path by the sea, which is the start of the **Essex Way**, a long distance path of 81 miles (130km) connecting Harwich with Epping. Pass **Harwich Town Sailing Club** and maintain direction along the **Esplanade** where at low tide you can walk along the shingle beach.

② Pass the **Treadwheel Crane** on your right and continue along the seafront taking care along the sloping concrete walkway. Keep the raised, fenced area of **Beacon Hill Fort** and the gun emplacements from World War One and World War Two to your right. As you pass the breakwaters around the bay there are views of the holiday resort of Dovercourt. Ignore the steps to your right and continue along the **Essex Way**, walking parallel with the upper road of **Marine Parade** on your right.

> **WHAT TO LOOK FOR**
> Look for two quite different walls. One is the Flint Wall in Kings Head Street, made from ship's ballast, and the other is the remains of the 12th-century **town wall**. The latter is in St Nicholas' Churchyard, opposite the vestry door, where at ground level you can see part of a wall built of septaria, a poor quality stone dredged out of the local estuaries.

③ Turn right into **Lower Marine Parade** and pass the **War Memorial and Gardens** at the junction with Fronk's Road and Marine Parade. Maintain direction passing the **Cliff Hotel** on the left and then go left into **Kingsway**, opposite the statue of Queen Victoria. Turn right into the **High Street** and bear left into **Main Road**, passing the police station on your left. Walk for 250yds (229m) and turn right up the track to see the **Redoubt**, a

> **WHILE YOU'RE THERE**
> Visit St Nicholas' Church built of pale yellow brick in simple Gothic style. Crusaders prayed here before leaving for their journey to the Holy Land; royalty worshipped here on their way to the Continent; and other luminaries, such as Willoughby, Drake, Nelson, Samuel Pepys and Daniel Defoe almost certainly dropped in when they lodged at Harwich.

Martello-style fort, part of the defences against Napoleonic invasion. Continue to pass **Cox's Pond**, once owned by local bankers of the same name. They are better known in military circles as Cox and Kings, the Army bankers.

④ Pass **High Lighthouse** on the right, turn right into **Wellington Road** and left into **Church Street** passing St Nicholas' Church. Turn right into **Market Street** and left into **Kings Head Street**, pausing to admire the timber-framed Elizabethan houses including No 21, the home of Christopher Jones, captain of the *Mayflower*.

⑤ Turn right into **The Quay**, where Quayside Court faces the sea. Now a block of apartments, Quayside Court was built as one of the Great Eastern hotels in the 19th century and catered for travellers from the Continent who would arrive by steamer at what is now Trinity Quay and continue their journey to London by rail.

> **WHERE TO EAT AND DRINK** ⓘ
> There are plenty of pubs to choose from, many dating back to the 16th and 17th centuries. Options include the Globe in Kings Quay Street one of the oldest buildings in Harwich, the Angel Inn and the Ship Restaurant next to the shipyard and the Alma Inn, a former wealthy merchant's house.

Manningtree – England's Smallest Town

Where the Witchfinder General was born and buried and a Site of Special Scientific Interest.

•DISTANCE•	7 miles (11.3km)
•MINIMUM TIME•	3hrs 30min
•ASCENT / GRADIENT•	98ft (30m) ▲▲▲
•LEVEL OF DIFFICULTY•	👫 👫 👫
•PATHS•	Field paths, footpaths, tracks and sections of road, may be boggy, 5 stiles
•LANDSCAPE•	River estuary, undulating farmland dotted with woodland and residential areas
•SUGGESTED MAP•	aqua3 OS Explorer 184 Colchester, Harwich & Clacton-on-Sea
•START / FINISH•	Grid reference: TM 093322
•DOG FRIENDLINESS•	Can romp free in woodland but must be on lead on farmland and in town
•PARKING•	Pay-and-display at Manningtree Station; free at weekends
•PUBLIC TOILETS•	Manningtree Station

BACKGROUND TO THE WALK

On the banks of the River Stour, Manningtree and neighbouring Mistley have long been associated with mills, maltings and timber. In 1753, ships for the Napoleonic Wars were built at Mistley Quay, and Newcastle coal, Scandinavian timber, grain, bricks, chalk, flour and hay were brought down river and transported by barge to London. But these tiny towns, separated by a few miles, are possessed of a darker side... witches!

Matthew Hopkins – Witchfinder General

Cast your mind back to the bad old days of 1644 and imagine reputed witches fleeing from Manningtree's most infamous resident, Matthew Hopkins, better known as the Witchfinder General. If you were female and happened to own a black cat, you risked being branded a witch, to be hunted down by Hopkins' band of distinctly unmerry men. Securing a conviction for witchcraft on the flimsiest of evidence was Hopkins' stock-in-trade, a profession made more unpalatable by the fact that Parliament paid him 20 shillings for each 'guilty' witch. The fate of Hopkins himself is in dispute. Some believe he died a peaceful death at his home in Manningtree in 1647, while others say he was eventually subjected to one of his own witchfinding tests, was found guilty and sentenced to death accordingly. He is believed to be buried in St Mary's Church at Mistley.

This walk starts from Manningtree Station overlooking the River Stour, which separates Essex from Suffolk, and rises to 14th-century St Mary's Church at Lawford to join the Essex Way. It crosses undulating meadows and thick forest, perfect territory for fleeing witches. A green lane emerges at Mistley where the Swan Fountain is the last surviving example of landowner Richard Rigby's attempts to turn the area into a fashionable spa.

By the end of the 17th century, Mistley and Manningtree were flourishing, busy ports. Malting, Mistley's oldest industry, took off too, and you can still see the chimneys of the English Diastatic Malt Extract Company (EDME) factory on this walk. If you follow the River Stour, through a Site of Special Scientific Interest (SSSI), back to Manningtree you may spot a large colony of swans, attracted by the waste of the maltings, and other estuary birds including shelduck, teal and ringed plover.

At Manningtree, many of the roof beams of the delightful shops and houses in the High Street date back to Elizabethan times. The witches are long gone, or so they say, and it's hard to believe that between 1644 and 1646 up to 300 victims were rounded up in these parts. Hopkins sometimes held court at local inns, but most of his victims were sent for trial at the notorious Chelmsford Assizes, and many were tried on the evidence of children. Those found guilty were either burnt at the stake or hanged, some of them here on Manningtree's tiny green.

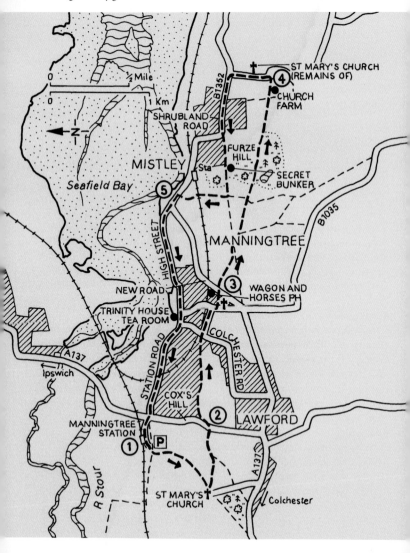

Walk 2

Walk 2 Directions

① From the car park turn right at the **Dedham** fingerpost following the sign for **Lawford** on a steep, grassy path to **St Mary's Church**. Go through the black gate and, keeping the church on your right, cross the stile over the church wall. Turn left and, at the wooden post, follow the yellow waymark half right across the meadow. Cross the earth bridge over **Wignell Brook**, then go left uphill keeping the line of trees on your right. Just before the house at the top of the hill, cross the stile and bear left to **Cox's Hill**, on to the A137.

② Cross **Cox's Hill**, turn left and after 40yds (37m), at a fingerpost marking the **Essex Way**, turn right. Walk downhill with trees on your left and a pond on your right. Pass the housing estate on your left and cross the plank bridge over a stream. Follow the gravel path through the **Owl Conservation Area**. Ignoring the concrete path on the left, turn half right on to the cross-field path towards playing fields. Cross **Colchester Road**, and at the T-junction turn right into **Trinity Road**, ignoring signs for the Essex Way. At the Evangelical church turn left between houses to **New Road**, the **Wagon and Horses** pub is on the left.

③ Cross **New Road** and follow the yellow waymarked footpath between backs of houses. At the T-junction turn left on to the wide canopied bridleway. After 70yds (64m) follow the waymark half right and rejoin the **Essex Way**. Maintain direction, crossing an earth bridge over the brook followed by two stiles. Just after the second stile, follow the track between two concrete posts into the thickly wooded slopes of **Furze Hill**. As you emerge from the woods, go straight ahead keeping to the field-edge path to **Church Farm**. Turn left here on to **Heath Road**.

> ### WHAT TO LOOK FOR ⓘ
> In Manningtree look for fine examples of **weavers' cottages** in Brook Street and South Street and, suspended against a tower, an effigy of the **Manningtree Ox**, immortalised in Shakespeare's *Henry IV*.

④ Cross the road to the low wall to see the remains of **St Mary's Church**. Continue north and turn left on to the B1352 and into **Shrubland Road** which soon becomes a green lane. Cross the first stile on the right and walk under the railway. Turn left into **Mistley Green** which joins the **High Street**.

⑤ Turn left at the **High Street**, and follow **The Walls** beside the River Stour into **Manningtree**. Turn left into the **High Street** and continue for a mile (1.6km) along **Station Road** to the car park.

> ### WHERE TO EAT AND DRINK ⓘ
> Halfway through the walk, in Manningtree itself, you can stop for lunch and a refreshing pint at the **Wagon and Horses** in New Road. Vegetarian options and a good selection of teas can be had at **Trinity House Tea Room** in the High Street – the profits go to a local initiative called Acorn Village, which helps people with disabilities.

> ### WHILE YOU'RE THERE ⓘ
> Visit the cold war operations centre at Mistley's **secret bunker**, just before the green lane to Manningtree. In the bunker, built in 1951 half above and half below ground, you can experience sound effects, watch a video and learn how Essex would react in a nuclear attack.

Walk 3

Waltzing Around Walton-on-the-Naze

A day beside the Essex coast exploring a town with two seasides.

•DISTANCE•	4¼ miles (6.8km)
•MINIMUM TIME•	2hrs
•ASCENT / GRADIENT•	Negligible
•LEVEL OF DIFFICULTY•	
•PATHS•	Grassy cliff paths, tidal salt marsh and some town streets
•LANDSCAPE•	Cliffs, sandy beaches, creeks and marshes
•SUGGESTED MAP•	aqua3 OS Explorer 184 Colchester, Harwich & Clacton-on-Sea
•START / FINISH•	Grid reference: TM 253218
•DOG FRIENDLINESS•	The ozone drives dogs a little mad so take care on narrow paths along cliffs
•PARKING•	Pay-and-display at Mill Lane and Naze Tower
•PUBLIC TOILETS•	Mill Lane and Naze Tower

BACKGROUND TO THE WALK

In the early 19th century Walton-le-Soken, as Walton-on-the-Naze was then known, emerged as a seaside resort attracting fashionable folk from London and county families from Essex, who used bathing machines to dip their toes in the waters. The first terraced houses brought genteel residents, a hotel provided visitors with accommodation and before long the area became as popular as Southend with a pier packed with pastimes. Although Walton's name has since changed, two neighbouring villages, Kirby-le-Soken and Thorpe-le-Soken, still retain the original suffix.

Holiday Resort and Wildlife Haven

Nowadays visitors can enjoy amusement arcades, tenpin bowling, restaurants and sea fishing, and the holiday atmosphere is complete with kiss-me-quick hats, jellied eels and seaside rock. But if you wander north of the town and its lovely wide sandy beaches, you'll discover a haven for bird life in the John Weston Nature Reserve, named after a local warden, and a multitude of sailing craft tucked in the creeks.

Under Threat from Erosion

Part of the town is situated on a headland called The Naze, hence its name. The word originates from the Anglo-Saxon 'ness' or 'naes' meaning a headland, while Walton may mean 'walled town' from the sea wall. Natural erosion has played a big part in the development of Walton-on-the-Naze, although some would class it as terrifying destruction. In 1798 Walton's second church was washed away and at low tide they say you can still hear the bell ring; in 1880 its first pier was destroyed by heavy seas; World War Two gun emplacements and pillboxes built on the Naze itself fell on to the beach and in the next few years, the Naze Tower, a Grade II listed building, which is only just 100yds (91m) from the cliff edge will also be at risk.

Conservationists predict that unless coastal erosion is stopped, or at least slowed down to managable levels, then the area known as the Walton backwaters and home to thousands of birds, seals and other wildlife, will disappear along with a large part of Walton itself. It may come as no surprise that even the lifeboat here lacks a permanent mooring. In fact it is the only lifeboat in Britain to have a mooring in the open sea. It is near the end of the pier and, when the alarm is raised, the lifeboat crew cycle the length of the pier and use a small launch to reach it.

Choose a summer's day for this gentle walk, which takes you through the town and along the seafront to the Naze Tower. You can walk along the beach or along the promenade depending on the tidal conditions. Year round, Walton-on-the-Naze is a delight to explore. In winter you'll see waders and a range of wildfowl, including brent geese and, in summer, you may be lucky to spot rare avocets, which breed here. They have unusual upturned bills which they sweep through the water collecting shrimps and worms.

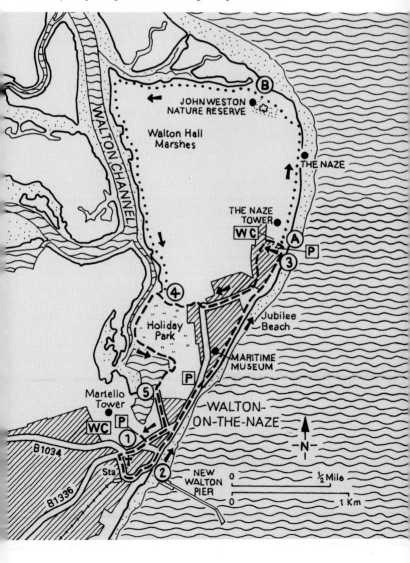

Walk 3

Walk 3 Directions

① From **Mill Lane car park** turn right into the **High Street** then left into **Martello Street**. Bear left along **New Pier Street** and go on to **Pier Approach**. To your right is the Pier, its ½ mile (800m) length makes it the second longest in England, after Southend. From here there are good views of the beaches of Walton-on-the-Naze and Frinton.

WHAT TO LOOK FOR

You can see the **geological structure** of the cliffs from small promontories or from the beach. At the top of the cliffs the boulder clay and gravel date from the Ice Age. Below are red crag and the slippery grey deposits of London clay, which at the bottom look like brown flakes. Sand martins nest here.

---

② Turn left and, with the sea on your right, walk along **Princes Esplanade** through **East Terrace** at the end of which is the **Maritime Museum**. Continue walking along **Cliff Parade** and the cliff tops to **Naze Tower**. Built by Trinity House in 1720 as a navigational aid, it was to join many Martello towers which were constructed along the east and south east coasts of England to fend off Napoleonic invasion. Nowadays, the grassy area in which the tower stands is a good place to rest and recuperate with a hot drink and a picnic at the wooden tables.

WHILE YOU'RE THERE

Call in at the **Maritime Museum** and see the exhibits relating to Frinton and Walton's close association with the sea and farming. This former lifeboat house also has displays on lifeboat history, including snippets on how the local lifeboat was regularly called out to pirate radio ships in distress in the 1960s.

---

③ From the car park café walk inland to **Old Hall Lane**, turn left and then right into **Naze Park Road**. At the end of Naze Park Road, where it bears sharp left, turn right on to the narrow path and left on to the field-edge path passing two small ponds filled with wildlife.

④ After 100yds (91m), turn left on to the cross path, go through the gate and on to the permissive path which follows the sea wall, keeping the caravan site on your left and **Walton Channel** on your right. This wide expanse of mudflats, islands, channels and small boats, ever changing with the tide, is a paradise for seabirds and a Site of Special Scientific Interest (SSSI). Skippers Island, an Essex Wildlife Trust nature reserve, is the habitat of rare seabirds and wildlife and full-time wardens are employed to protect them. Follow the sea wall for ¾ mile (1.2km) then bear half left down the embankment and into the field.

⑤ Walk 70yds (64m) to a path between the primary school playing field and houses and enter **Saville Street** past a row of old cottages on your right. Take the first right into **North Street**, continue to the **High Street** and turn right. Turn right again into **Mill Lane** and return to the car park.

WHERE TO EAT AND DRINK

There are lots of cafés, fast food and fish and chip shops along the Esplanade and in the High Street. Open year round is **Grandma's** in Newgate Street, a delightful low-ceilinged restaurant offering steak and kidney pie and other treats. The **Victory** pub is next door while **White's** offers pie and mash and jellied or stewed eels. A snack bar beside Naze Tower keeps hungry walkers happy too.

The Salt Marshes and Seabirds of Hamford Water

A longer loop walk taking in an exhilarating cliff path and nature reserve.
See map and information panel for Walk 3

•**DISTANCE**•	6¼ miles (10.1km)
•**MINIMUM TIME**•	3hrs
•**ASCENT / GRADIENT**•	Negligible
•**LEVEL OF DIFFICULTY**•	🚶🚶 🚶🚶 🚶🚶

Walk 4 Directions (Walk 3 option)

From the car park by the **Naze Tower**, Point Ⓐ, follow the path along the cliff edge, though not too close as it is rapidly eroding. In recent years the weather and tides have caused the local red clay and shingle to slide away from the flaky London clay underbed. Much of this can be seen if, at low tide, you take the path along the beach; this is also the route for fossil finds. It's easy to ignore the problems of erosion when you look around at the raw natural beauty of this meeting of wild land and open sea.

Back on the cliff top, continue along the path past large clumps of elder scrub and gorse bush where you may catch a glimpse of small birds such as linnets and goldfinches. As the path slopes downhill the wide Stour estuary comes into view, with Harwich and Felixstowe in the distance. Be careful here, the path nears the cliff edge with gorse on your left, but in another 100yds (91m) the path reaches sea level where there is access to the beach and, particularly at low tide, mudflats and rock pools – a haven for small children and their grandparents.

Follow the path uphill along the grassy bank of the new sea wall. To your right you can see the remains of the old sea wall, an indication of the level of erosion in recent years. After 300yds (274m) on the landward side, you can see the enclosed area of the Essex Wildlife Trust's **John Weston Nature Reserve**, Point Ⓑ. The embankment provides a fine vantage point to observe the comings and goings of migrating birds. From here on the area is virtually a bird domain. All through the year terns and waders nest on the beaches and the local redshank and shelduck nest on the salt marshes of Hamford Water. This great conservation area stretches as far as the eye can see, across saltings, marshes and islands, some of which are protected by wardens and one of which, Horsey, is inhabited, but is only accessible at low water.

Your walk continues with this vista for 1¼ miles (2km) until you reach the cross path by **Foundry Lane** to rejoin the Walk 3 at Point ④.

Walk 5

Colchester – Britain's Oldest Recorded Town

Following Romans and Victorians along Colchester's ancient walls.

•DISTANCE•	3 miles (4.8km)
•MINIMUM TIME•	1hr 30min
•ASCENT / GRADIENT•	33ft (10m)
•LEVEL OF DIFFICULTY•	
•PATHS•	Town streets
•LANDSCAPE•	Castle, town and park
•SUGGESTED MAP•	aqua3 OS Explorer 184 Colchester, Harwich & Clacton-on-Sea
•START / FINISH•	Grid reference: TM 001253
•DOG FRIENDLINESS•	Museums, castles and shopping centres aren't usually a dog's idea of a good time
•PARKING•	Pay-and-display car parks in city centre
•PUBLIC TOILETS•	Castle Park beside Hollytrees Museum

Walk 5 Directions

Imagine yourself back in AD 43 as a lonely Briton trudging across the south east landscape when you spot a huge Roman army marching towards you. They descend on your home town, which they call 'Camulodunum', and before you know it, they make it the capital of Roman Britain endowing it with a theatre, temples and large houses with central heating and running water. Within a few years a fearsome queen called Boudica turns up with her army and razes the lot to the ground before continuing to London and St Albans. The Romans rebuild the town within a thick defensive wall.

Today Camulodunum is Colchester, a modern town on the A12, sited on the old Roman road which crossed what was to become Essex from the south west to the north east and continued to Harwich on the coast. There's little left of those grand houses and the Roman temple is buried beneath Britain's oldest Norman castle in the heart of town, but much of the Roman wall remains. On this walk you can trace the old wall, taking in snippets of Colchester's colourful history along the way.

From the car park, keep the wall on your left and follow it along **Priory Road** to **East Hill**. Turn left and walk to the top of the hill. Here is the keep of Colchester Castle surrounded by the lovely grounds

WHILE YOU'RE THERE

Take a guided tour of the **castle** and visit the foundations, dungeons and ramparts or let the children play with 'touchy feeley' boxes containing pottery and other surprises which give an insight into what life was like in Roman times. Adults may enjoy the fragrance of the **Sensory Gardens** in Castle Park.

of Castle Park. Walk through the park keeping the castle on your left and note the obelisk at the rear, which marks the site of execution in 1648 of two aristocratic upstarts, Sir Charles Lucas and Sir George Lisle, who lay siege to the town during the Civil War.

With the castle still on your left, take the first exit and turn right into **Madenburgh Street**, where amidst a row of terraced Victorian houses, at No 74, are the remains of the Roman theatre viewable through a glass panel. Continue walking downhill and turn left into **Northgate Street**, formerly known as Dutch Lane. In the 16th century, Dutch Protestants fleeing persecution at home, settled here and brought their weaving skills with them. You can see some fine examples of these timber-framed houses on the corner of West Stockwell Street.

At the end of Northgate Street, turn left into **North Hill** passing the timber-framed **Ye Old Marquis** inn and a row of 18th-century houses. A little way along on the same side of the road, stop and admire St Peter's parish church with its Victorian clock. Wealthy Victorian merchants improved churches, built new ones and generally contributed to the town's prosperity with the construction of Castle Park, a

public library and schools. Walk straight on to **Head Street** keeping the High Street on your left. After 200yds (183m) posts on the left indicate Sir Isaac's Walk, a pedestrianised area of specialist shops leading to the town centre. Turn left into **Trinity Street** with its Elizabethan timber-framed cottages and stop at Tymperly's Clock Museum. This early 15th-century house, one of the oldest in the town, was the residence of William Gilberd, physician to Queen Elizabeth I in 1601.

At the end of Trinity Street is the Holy Trinity Church, with its Saxon tower, still standing after 1,000 years and incongruously surrounded by the modern shopping precinct. Turn right here into **Culver Street West** and follow the fingerposts into **Lion Walk** where the United Reformed church, with its 17th-century portal, stands at ground level while the remainder of the church is hidden above shops.

Keeping the church on your left, turn left again into **Eld Lane** where a lift leads to the market (open Friday and Saturday) and car park. Peer over the side and you will see that you are on the old city walls. Take the lift or walk down the steps and continue along **Vineyard Street** where you can pick up the old wall again on your left.

You are now outside the wall. Cross **St Botolph's Street** into **Priory Street** where you'll see the remains of 12th-century **St Botolph's Priory**, a good example of early recycling by craftsmen who, due to the absence of suitable building material, used the remains of Roman buildings. Turn right and return to the car park.

Bracing Bradwell-on-Sea

Smugglers, sea walls and a dying nuclear power station.

•DISTANCE•	6 miles (9.7km)
•MINIMUM TIME•	3hrs
•ASCENT / GRADIENT•	Negligible
•LEVEL OF DIFFICULTY•	
•PATHS•	Stony and grassy paths with some road walking
•LANDSCAPE•	Mudflats, salt marshes, beach, farmland, sea wall and nuclear power station
•SUGGESTED MAP•	aqua3 OS Explorer 176 Blackwater Estuary, Maldon
•START / FINISH•	Grid reference: TM 024078
•DOG FRIENDLINESS•	A beach for a good romp and paddle; nuclear power station provides a poop bin
•PARKING•	Informal parking at entrance to footpath at East Hall Farm and free car park at Bradwell Nuclear Power Station
•PUBLIC TOILETS•	Visitor Centre at Bradwell Nuclear Power Station

BACKGROUND TO THE WALK

If you yearn for huge skies, bracing sea air and long yellow sands, with not a lilo or brolly in sight, then this walk is for you. The Dengie (sounds like Benjie) Peninsula, a vast area of pancake-flat marshes and arable farmland, really does seem in a world of its own, its haunting beauty attracting those seeking to escape the stresses of modern city life.

Smugglers' Haunts

The Dengie Peninsula is bounded by the estuaries of the River Blackwater to the north and the River Crouch to the south. Yet for all its isolation, jutting out into the dove-grey waters of the North Sea, it was a place that needed defending. The Romans built a fort where the present Chapel of St Peter's-on-the-Wall stands, one of several along the coast built to fend off raiders. In the 18th and 19th centuries the chapel took on a different role as a hiding place for bands of smugglers, who would use it to store crates of whisky and rum and other contraband. Meanwhile, notable Bradwell residents, such as Hezekiah Staines, played part-time policeman by day and criminal by night, and spread rumours that the chapel was haunted. Maybe it is.

Contraband Course

This walk starts on an isolated pathway leading to the Chapel of St Peter's-on-the-Wall, the oldest church still in use in England and certainly the sole monument to Celtic Christianity in Essex. Built by the missionary St Cedd in AD 654 it is almost entirely made from debris from the Roman fort on which it stands. In 1920 it took on its present name, and since 1948 has attracted pilgrims from all over the world. Each summer, services are held in the simple barn-like interior. If you choose to take this walk on a cold winter's day when the skies are white and the mists cast a ghostly shroud over the bleak windswept marshes, it's a perfect place for taking shelter from the elements. Once through the heavy wooden door you can imagine old smugglers stacking up their ill-gotten goods inside.

Walk 6

Perhaps the most incongruous blot on the landscape, as you continue along the sea wall to Bradwell Waterside, are the looming grey, grim blocks of Bradwell Nuclear Power Station, visible for miles around. It started life in 1962, but costs of continued operation now outweigh its earning potential, and the site is due to be decommissioned. You can take refreshment at the Green Man pub, a smugglers' haven in its day, before continuing to Bradwell-on-Sea, in truth a good way from the seaside. And to complete the contraband course, pause at the parish church where miscreants were incarcerated in a tiny square cell, the Cage, or punished at the whipping post.

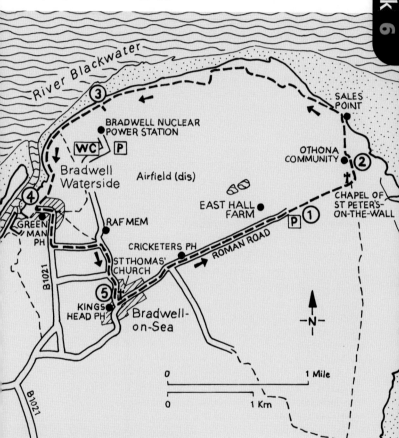

Walk 6 Directions

① Take the wide grassy path from the car park towards the sea and in ½ mile (800m) reach the ancient **Chapel of St Peter's-on-the-Wall**. Continue walking towards the sea for another 30yds (27m) and turn left at the T-junction. After 100yds (91m) climb the wooden steps to the sea defence wall.

② At the fingerpost marking the religious community of Othona, turn right and walk along the wall with the sea on your right. For the next 2 miles (3.2km) your route remains on top of the sea wall, mainly a firm, grassy path

Walk 6

punctuated with areas of concrete. On your left, and sometimes seemingly at a lower level to the sea, is private farmland. On your right, salt marsh gives way to white sand and shingle and extensive mudflats at low tide. The seashore makes a lovely detour but at high tide you have to remain on the concrete path. There are good views across the Blackwater estuary to Mersea Island. On the seaward side of the path there are concrete pill boxes, relics of World War Two. The second pill box marks **Sales Point**, from where there are views of the mooring area used by Thames sailing barges. Follow the path for a mile (1.6km) and you can see the framework of the beacon, a good place for spotting swooping cormorants.

> ### WHILE YOU'RE THERE
> Call in at British Nuclear Fuels Limited's Visitor Centre at **Bradwell Nuclear Power Station**. Here you can find out all about electricity production, nuclear generation and decommissioning and the environmental aspects of supplying the world with energy. Telephone in advance for full details of their opening hours on 01621 873395.

③ In 1½ miles (2.4km) the bulk of **Bradwell Nuclear Power Station** is upon you. You may either continue on the route by the coast or make a detour to take in the nature trail around the station and/or call at the **Visitor Centre**. Our route continues along the sea wall to **Bradwell Waterside**.

④ At the jetty, turn left on to **Waterside Road** keeping the yacht club and **Green Man** pub on your

> ### WHERE TO EAT AND DRINK
> A rather limited choice confined to public houses. Take your pick from the **Cricketers** in Roman Road, the **Green Man** at Bradwell Waterside, or the **Kings Head** at Bradwell-on-Sea which has displays of old photographs of the area and a pair of llamas in the backyard to amuse the children.

right. Continue along **Waterside Road** with the marina on your right. Sean Connery, Bobby Moore and Roger Moore had a hand in turning this marina into a business venture in the 1960s. Continue past the marina and turn left into **Trusses Road**. At the T-junction, turn right towards **Bradwell-on-Sea** (a left turn here towards Bradwell Nuclear Power Station will take you to the RAF memorial at Bradwell Bay Airfield).

⑤ At Bradwell-on-Sea follow the **High Street** to its junction with **East End Road** where, on the corner, you will find St Thomas' Church opposite the **Kings Head** pub. Pass **Caidge Cottages** on your left, the village school on your right and continue for about a mile (1.6km) along the straight **Roman Road**, with maybe a stop at the **Cricketers** pub, before reaching the car park.

> ### WHAT TO LOOK FOR
> Look for the **war memorial** beside the disused airfield perimeter track at Bradwell-on-Sea. Surrounded by remembrance poppies, it is in the form of a battleship grey Mosquito aircraft appearing to plunge into the ground and is a poignant reminder of those pilots who never returned from operations during World War Two.

Paddling up Paglesham Creek

A stroll along the sea wall from Paglesham Eastend to Paglesham Churchend, in the footsteps of smugglers, 'wife-farmers' and oyster fishermen.

•DISTANCE•	6¼ miles (10.1km)
•MINIMUM TIME•	2hrs 45min
•ASCENT / GRADIENT•	Negligible
•LEVEL OF DIFFICULTY•	
•PATHS•	Grassy sea wall, field edge, unmade tracks, 5 stiles
•LANDSCAPE•	River estuary, salt marsh, mudflats, grazing and arable farmland
•SUGGESTED MAP•	aqua3 OS Explorer 176 Blackwater Estuary, Maldon
•START / FINISH•	Grid reference: TQ 943922
•DOG FRIENDLINESS•	Big skies and lots of water, but keep on lead along sea wall, where sheep are grazing.
•PARKING•	Informal street parking at Paglesham Eastend beside Plough and Sail Inn
•PUBLIC TOILETS•	None on route

BACKGROUND TO THE WALK

Paglesham, just a few miles from Southend-on-Sea, is bordered to the north by the River Crouch and to the south by the River Roach. Its origins go back to Saxon times and its population survived mainly by rearing sheep that grazed on the flat marshlands. But its remote position on Essex's east coast, and its proximity to waterways, attracted smugglers who would sail up the river bringing in their ill-gotten gains to pass on at a profit to anyone who was happy to make some easy money.

Brazen Blyth

Smuggling was such big business that at one time the entire population of Paglesham was involved in one way or another. In the 18th century one famous resident, William Blyth – also known as Hard-Apple Blyth – was considered to be one of the most notorious smugglers Paglesham ever produced. He started out as the village grocer, progressed to churchwarden and was reputed to have torn up church records to use as wrapping for his butter and bacon. Brazen Blyth would not only evade Customs officials but his party piece was spending evenings at the Punch Bowl pub drinking whole kegs of brandy and crunching wine glasses. This unusual diet and lifestyle clearly did him no harm. He died in 1830, aged 74, and was buried at Paglesham church.

Wife and Oyster Farming

'Wife-farming' seems to have been another popular pastime. Daniel Defoe, in his travels around Paglesham, noted that some men boasted that they had fifteen or more wives. Stories circulated at the time that the women who couldn't stand the rigorous lifestyle and bad weather here, either died from the cold or abandoned their more robust husbands for a more comfortable existence in the uplands from where they originally came. The men simply chose a replacement.

When the villagers weren't smuggling or 'wife-farming' they were engaged in oyster farming, a lucrative business which peaked in the mid-19th century. Oysters were considered common food for Londoners who couldn't get enough of them, and the shortage provided the people of Paglesham with plenty of work. Scores of fishermen would sail out along the estuaries of the Crouch and Roach and return to have their oysters processed by one of the big companies, such as the Roach River Company, now long gone.

On this walk you will see sheep grazing along the grassy sea wall and marshland, just as they have done for centuries, but you'll have to look hard for smugglers in the creeks and estuaries. Oysters are still farmed locally and an annual oyster festival brings a flurry of foodies to the pubs.

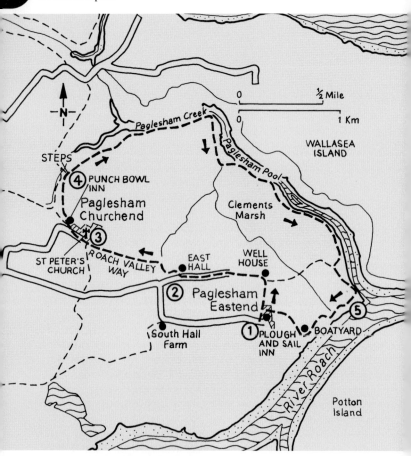

Walk 7 Directions

① Walk to the left of the **Plough and Sail Inn** along a driveable track, and after 100yds (91m)

follow the fingerpost straight ahead to the left of the house called **Cobblers Row**. Maintain direction along a good field-edge path, with arable fields either side, until the path narrows and you approach

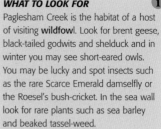

Walk 7

towards the River Crouch where you have views of the marinas of Burnham-on-Crouch and the warehouses and timber yards of Wallasea Island. Much of the landward side of the embankment is given over to sheep grazing which makes this walk somewhat difficult for larger dogs as enclosures are often divided by wooden stiles and low voltage electric fencing.

houses in the distance. Keeping the red brick wall on your left go through the white wicket gate, with the brook on your right, and along the lawn of **Well House**. Go through another wicket gate and turn left on to the permissive path which becomes an unmade road.

② At the corrugated barn of **East Hall**, follow the **Roach Valley waymark**, right and then left, and maintain direction along the good, grassy field edge. Walk by paddock fencing, with Church Hall on your right and the pond on your left, to **St Peter's Church** at **Paglesham Churchend**.

③ Keeping the church on your right, continue along **Churchend High Street** to the **Punch Bowl Inn**. Maintain direction for 50yds (46m), take the concrete path to your right and after a few paces follow the **Roach Valley waymark**, left, which soon becomes a grassy field-edge path running parallel with a waterway on your left.

④ Take a short clamber up the grassy embankment and, leaving the **Roach Valley Way**, turn right on to the sea wall of **Paglesham Creek**. Keep to the path as it meanders by Paglesham Creek, which widens as you approach the River Roach. To your left the salt marshes stretch

⑤ As the path bears right, with the river on your left, maintain direction past oyster beds until you reach the boatyard. Go down the steps from the sea wall and pick your way through boats and machinery to the gate. Squeeze through the gate and follow the unmade track until you pass a row of cottages on your left, followed by **Cobblers Row** and the fingerpost on your right that was the direction for the outward journey. Turn left and return to the Plough and Sail Inn at **Paglesham Eastend**.

Walk 8

A Meander Through Maldon

Combine historic Maldon, home of salt making, with a network of fascinating waterways.

•DISTANCE•	4¼ miles (6.8km)
•MINIMUM TIME•	2hrs
•ASCENT / GRADIENT•	113ft (35m)
•LEVEL OF DIFFICULTY•	
•PATHS•	Mainly grassy paths, narrow in parts and prone to mud after rain, some roads, 5 stiles
•LANDSCAPE•	River estuary, some woodland, canal tow path, marshland and mudflats, some urban streets
•SUGGESTED MAP•	aqua3 OS Explorer 183 Chelmsford & The Rodings, Maldon & Witham
•START / FINISH•	Grid reference: TL 853070
•DOG FRIENDLINESS•	Lots of water but dogs shouldn't take a dip, they could get stuck in mud. Watch out for Shetland ponies too
•PARKING•	Pay-and-display car park at Butts Lane
•PUBLIC TOILETS•	Butt Lane

BACKGROUND TO THE WALK

Top television chefs swear by the healthy attributes of sea salt and keen cooks will notice that they often refer to Maldon Sea Salt in their culinary creations. In this walk you'll not only discover picturesque pathways, historic buildings and estuarine bird life, but also pass the factory which has been the home of salt manufacturing since 1882.

A Victorious Battle

Salt aside, it's hard to imagine that the rural riverside town of Maldon, perched on a hill above the River Chelmer, was once the scene of a bloody battle. But one morning, back in AD 991, the Saxon inhabitants awoke to witness 93 Viking longboats sailing up the estuary of the River Blackwater. The invaders, hell-bent on death, destruction and victory, were forced to camp at Northey Island, thanks to a receding tide which left their ships stranded. Word had spread that Sandwich and Ipswich had already been plundered, and under the leadership of Byrhtnoth, Maldon's heroic leader, a two-day battle on the marshes opposite Northey Island ended in a Saxon victory. Poor Byrhtnoth, however, died on the battlefield, his head carried off as a trophy.

Between the 17th and early 19th centuries Maldon thrived as a port town and centre of admiralty jurisdiction due to its position at the head of the Blackwater Estuary. In 1797 the Chelmer and Blackwater Navigation opened linking the town with Chelmsford. Although the town lost out on port dues and maritime trade declined, Maldon retained its prominence, with a flourishing oyster industry and barge trade. Indeed, it was second in importance only to Colchester, and had already established is own abbey, grammar school, library and Moot Hall, which later served as a police station, a court and a jail house.

Thanks to the popularity of salt water bathing in the 18th century and the growing barge trade from London, Maldon flourished. By 1847 the town was linked to London by rail and a promenade park attracted wealthy citizens. Ships still come up on the tide bringing grain from Holland to the flour mill on the banks of the River Chelmer and you can also see the traditional Thames sailing barges, identified by their red sails. Many are now given over to pleasure sailing, but in days gone by they plied their trade along the east coast to London.

Today this smart town, with its narrow streets and attractive timber-framed buildings, many with 18th- and 19th-century façades, welcomes the boating fraternity. Landlubbers, more interested in Maldon's social history rather than messing about in boats, can explore the pathways along the River Chelmer or the tow paths of the Chelmer and Blackwater Navigation, which meet in a complex of waterways at Beeleigh Falls.

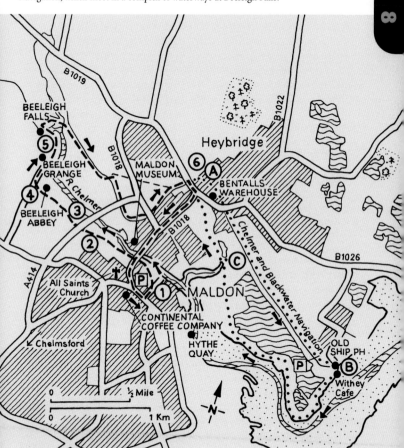

Walk 8 Directions

① From the car park turn left and walk towards **Downs Road**, keeping the houses on your left. The footpath drops quite steeply and soon you have views of the River Chelmer and the salt works. At the

riverside turn left, cross **Fullbridge** with care, and follow the grassy embankment keeping the river on your right. Maintain direction and cross two stiles separated by a concrete cross path. Follow the often muddy path, which meanders uphill through the sloping meadow usually occupied by horses.

Walk 8

② At the top of the hill turn right over the stile. Turn immediate right, along the downhill path through woodland and pass under the A414 **Maldon bypass**. Continue along the rising concrete path, and at the end turn right with the field (often with horses) on your left.

③ Maintain direction along the canopied green lane bounded by ancient hedgerows, keeping left to cross the stile. Follow the yellow waymark along the grassy path keeping left to emerge on to the gravel path via the timber gate.

> ### WHAT TO LOOK FOR ⓘ
> Mind your head at **Maldon's museum** in the old timbered building at Spindle's, just off the High Street. The museum is not giant-friendly, but shorties will find fascinating paintings, artefacts and portrayals of notable residents, including Maldon's celebrated 'fat' man, Edward Bright who, at the time of his death in 1750, weighed 44 stone (280kg).

④ On your right is **Beeleigh Abbey**. Continue past the abbey and at the end of the road turn right. Ignore the footpath on the left and pass **Beeleigh Grange Farm** on your left, and **Beeleigh Falls House**, an impressive Victorian villa, on the right. Go through the kissing gate and soon you hear the sound of rushing water of **Beeleigh Falls**.

⑤ Cross the timber bridge over the weir. At the end of the bridge turn right, keeping the river on your right. Stop at the second weir for good river views. Continue, keeping the river on your right, and go through the wooden kissing gate. At the canal lock turn right and walk, with the canal on your left, towards the red brick bridge. Do not cross

> ### WHILE YOU'RE THERE ⓘ
> Call in at the **Maeldune Heritage Centre** in the High Street and see the Maldon Embroidery, which depicts 1,000 years of the town's history, from the Battle of Maldon in 991 to its anniversary in 1991. It took 86 volunteer embroiderers three years to complete the seven panels, which form a total length of 42ft (13m).

the bridge, instead turn right on to the concrete path and then left on to the grassy path. Maintain direction with the canal on your left and the golf course on your right. Cross the next bridge and turn right, keeping the canal on your right. Continue under the **Maldon bypass** on to the grassy bridleway running parallel with the canal.

⑥ At the next bridge take the set of steps up to **Heybridge Street**. At the top turn right and join the **B1018** towards Maldon. Maintain direction to cross the River Chelmer via **Fullbridge**, bear left into **Market Hill**, turn left into the **High Street** and return to the car park via **Butt Lane** on your left.

> ### WHERE TO EAT AND DRINK ⓘ
> Dozens of eateries and pubs, many over 500 years old, line the High Street. Kick off with a croissant and cappuccino at the **Continental Coffee Company**, stop for a pie and a pint and views of Northey Island at the **Old Ship**, or tuck into bangers and chips at **Bunter's** mobile café opposite the now defunct Maldon East railway station.

Walk **9**

To Heybridge Basin

A longer loop walk taking in views of Northey Island and marshlands.
See map and information panel for Walk 8

•DISTANCE•	6½ miles (10.4km)
•MINIMUM TIME•	3hrs 30min
•ASCENT / GRADIENT•	113ft (35m) ▲▲ ▲ ▲
•LEVEL OF DIFFICULTY•	🚶🚶 🚶🚶 🚶🚶

Walk 9 Directions (Walk 8 option)

You can extend your walk along the canal to Heybridge Basin and see Northey Island, where in 991 Vikings camped before the Battle of Maldon. Cross **Heybridge Street**, Point Ⓐ, and rejoin the tow path along the Chelmer and Blackwater Navigation. On your left are the cemetery and canal gate. On your right are typical canalside buildings, including **Bentalls warehouse** built in 1863. William Bentall, a ploughmaker, transferred his business to Heybridge in 1805 to take advantage of the canal.

Walk along the tow path for 1 mile (1.6km), to **Heybridge Basin** where there are interesting 18th- and early 19th-century pubs and houses. This area replaced Fullbridge on the River Chelmer as the transhipment point for coal and other goods when the canal was completed. Today it is renowned for its expertise in converting barges and fishing boats into pleasure craft.

At the **Old Ship** public house, Point Ⓑ, turn right on to the footbridge over the lock and walk along the embankment. To your left is Northey Island and to your right, across marsh and heathland, are views of Maldon. Today Northey Island is a Site of Special Scientific Interest (SSSI), and can only be reached at low tide via a causeway. To the east is the privately-owned Osea Island, once rumoured to be a hideaway for celebrities.

As you continue towards the town look out for the spire of 12th-century **St Mary's Church**, which because of its location serves as a navigational aid for incoming shipping. Across the river you will see the attractive **Edwardian Park**, built in 1895 as a recreational centre for local people and visitors. To the right of the park is **Hythe Quay** where you'll see several Thames sailing barges with their characteristic sprit sail rigs. Their shallow draft allowed them to sail the muddy creeks and inlets of the Essex and Kent coasts but they became redundant following the development of road transport.

Follow the footpath for about 1 mile (1.6km), Point Ⓒ, to industrial installations on your left. Turn left here and immediately right along a grassy path which leads into **Bates Road**. After 500yds (457m) turn left in to the **B1018** to rejoin Walk 8.

Hadleigh Country Park

A fairly taxing walk with steep green slopes, marshes and a famous castle.

•DISTANCE•	4½ miles (7.2km)
•MINIMUM TIME•	2hrs 15min
•ASCENT / GRADIENT•	207ft (62m) ▲▲▲
•LEVEL OF DIFFICULTY•	🚶🚶🚶
•PATHS•	Woodland and field tracks, grassy paths and some streets
•LANDSCAPE•	Pasture and scrub, saltmarsh and woodland
•SUGGESTED MAP•	aqua3 OS Explorer 175 Southend-on-Sea & Basildon
•START / FINISH•	Grid reference: TQ 660874
•DOG FRIENDLINESS•	Plenty of open spaces but watch for cows around castle
•PARKING•	Free parking at Chapel Lane
•PUBLIC TOILETS•	Chapel Lane car park

Walk 10 Directions

Modern times may have engulfed much of Hadleigh's history, but in the village centre you can't fail to notice the 13th-century church enclosed, not by a green, but by a busy one-way traffic system. Meanwhile out on the hill overlooking the railway line, linking the Essex coast with London and beyond it the Thames estuary and the Kent countryside, are the ruins of Hadleigh Castle which stand as testimony to a bygone era. Founded by Hubert de Burgh in 1231 as a guard against the risk of attack by France, it was rebuilt by Edward III in the 14th century.

But before you visit the castle, take in part of **Hadleigh Country Park**. Start this walk from the car park and follow the path through the kissing gate. Turn left, taking the left stepped path downhill to a wide grassy plain, and make for the clump of trees on your right. At the fingerpost continue ahead crossing the road where the land rises gently.

Follow the path and you will see the railway line in the distance. Maintain this course, keeping the railway in view on your right, until you reach a waymarked path leading up to the castle.

Hadleigh Country Park has been an important conservation area since the 1950s due to its variety of habitats, from grassland and woodland to salt marsh and mudflat. The park covers 472 acres (191ha) and overlooks Canvey Island, the River Thames and the Kent Downs. The area once consisted of two farms, Poynetts and Kersey, which used only traditional chemical-free farming methods. The rich soil sustains a

> **WHILE YOU'RE THERE**
> Visit **Two Tree Island Nature Reserve** to the south east of the castle. Topsoil was brought in to cover this former rubbish dump, which today is a paradise for insects and small mammals. There is a bird hide overlooking the lagoon and marshland, which attract kingfishers, grey herons, avocets and short-eared owls and will appeal to twitchers.

Walk 10

variety of wildlife making this a delightful place to visit; in spring you can see shaded woodlands of bluebells, yellow calandine, nettle-like yellow archangel and plenty of butterflies; in summer you may hear the sound of a cuckoo or spot grass snakes and adders on the rough grass and heathland.

The views of the estuary and the Kent countryside improve with every step as you reach the summit of the hill, where you are greeted with the impressive remains of Hadleigh Castle. After Hubert de Burgh's death, in 1243, the danger of attack from France decreased and the castle fell into disrepair. They were spruced up again when Edward III came to the throne, in 1327. Huge sums were spent on importing stone and sand from Kent, chalk and plaster from London, wood and tiles from Thundersley, straw from Benfleet and glass from Rayleigh.

By 1551 the slopes were unstable and the castle suffered from landslip. It was sold to Lord Richard Riche who made a tidy sum selling the stone as building material for houses and churches on his extensive properties in Essex and by 1600 the castle was in ruins.

In the 19th century there were tales of a ghostly woman in white who dislocated the neck of a milkmaid

when she refused to meet her at midnight, and of smugglers who sailed up the River Thames, climbed the hill and hid their ill-gotten gains in the ruined castle. Such stories were told in the pubs in Hadleigh, where it was also believed that there was a tunnel linking Hadleigh Castle with the Castle Inn.

Having had your fill of folklore you now go through a kissing gate and turn right into **Castle Lane**, passing Home Farm, now a training centre for the Salvation Army. In 1890 General William Booth set up a colony here for the rehabilitation of down and outs from London. Some 400 men passed through the establishment, working at various aspects of farming, before either returning to their families, settling down in the local area or seeking pastures new via the Salvation Army's emigration department.

Walk up Castle Lane and at the top, where it meets the **High Street**, turn left. Cross the road to visit St James the Lesser Church with its lovely Norman apse. If it is open, look at the 13th-century carved font, but pride of place is taken by a painting of Thomas Becket. In the windows are modern portraits of Ethelburga, first Abbess of Barking.

Continue left along the **High Road**, passing the Waggon and Horses, turn left into **Chapel Lane** and return to the car park.

Walk 11

Rochford – the Place of the Peculiar People

An easy walk along the River Roach following part of the Roach Valley Way and a visit to a tiny medieval town.

•DISTANCE•	8 miles (12.9km)
•MINIMUM TIME•	3hrs
•ASCENT / GRADIENT•	Negligible
•LEVEL OF DIFFICULTY•	
•PATHS•	Grassy sea wall, field-edge paths and town streets
•LANDSCAPE•	River estuary, salt marsh, mudflats, arable land and urban development
•SUGGESTED MAP•	aqua3 OS Explorer 176 Blackwater Estuary, Maldon
•START / FINISH•	Grid reference: TQ 875904
•DOG FRIENDLINESS•	A big walk for many dogs with long sections on lead
•PARKING•	Pay-and-display at Back Lane
•PUBLIC TOILETS•	Back Lane car park

BACKGROUND TO THE WALK

Rochford, a small medieval market town, just over 3 miles (4.8km) north of Southend, is worth visiting before or after this walk for its abundance of delightful cottages, many of which are listed buildings. The town centre contains one of the few remaining market town cross patterns in England, comprising North, South, East and West Streets. In 1257, the lord of the manor, Sir Guy de Rochefort, was granted a charter to hold a weekly market, a tradition which still takes place every Tuesday in the attractive square.

But there have been horrific, and odd, goings-on in this peaceful town. In 1555 villagers gathered in the square to witness the execution of John Simson, a farm labourer from Great Wigborough. He was burnt at the stake because he refused to conform to Roman Catholicism. A plaque on the wall of a bakery shop commemorates his martyrdom.

Peculiar Experience

A few centuries later in 1837 James Banyard, a shoemaker, had a religious experience which inspired him to form a Christian sect which became known as the Peculiar People. Peculiar to Essex, the sect had its headquarters in Rochford. The group took its name from Deuteronomy, Chapter 14, Verse 2, which proclaims, 'and the Lord hath chosen thee to be a peculiar people unto himself'. Banyard, who took to religion after spending his life as a drunkard, rounded up followers and preached with such fervour that he and his flock were treated with suspicion and hostility.

Even more strange were their dress and customs. The men were clean shaven and wore bowler hats and the women went about their daily business in black bonnets. They rejected orthodox medicine and when one of the sect fell ill, the illness or disease was treated with the laying on of hands, or the affected part or parts would be anointed with oil. Needless to say, not all treatments were successful and there was often an outcry among local people when children from the sect died.

But in 1855, James Banyard's son became ill and, fearing that he would not live, Banyard summoned the doctor. Such disregard of the rules caused a split in the movement and Banyard was ousted. He was duly replaced and the centre of operations moved from Rochford to Daws Heath 5 miles (8km) away. Banyard never regained leadership and presumably went back to shoemaking; he died in 1863.

On this walk you may glimpse the ghost of a black-bonneted lady with her black skirts billowing like a sail on the flat open landscapes. She may disappear as soon as you hear the planes roaring above open fields bound for Southend Airport and if you linger long enough, she may re-appear. There are many peculiar happenings in this peculiar little town.

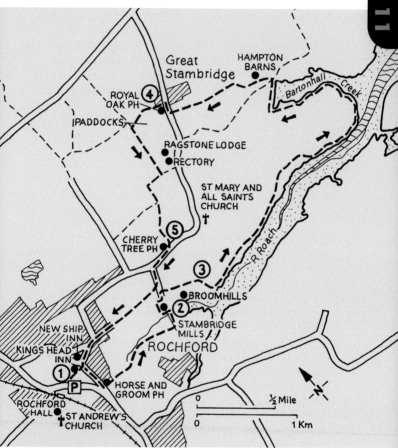

Walk 11 Directions

① From the car park walk north between houses into **Market Square** and turn right into **South Street**, passing the police station on your left. By the **Horse and Groom** pub, turn left into **Watts Lane** following

the **Roach Valley Way** through industrial installations and keeping the River Roach on your left for a mile (1.6km).

② Follow the path over the bridge, with **Stambridge Mill** straight ahead. Follow the concrete path around the mill until you reach

Walk 11

Mill Lane. Turn left, and after 50yds (46m), turn right on to the cross-field path to the footbridge over the fishing lake. Go through the kissing gate and on to the gravel path. Maintain direction through trees and across the meadow, where on your right you can see Broomhills house, the former home of John Harriot the founder of the Thames River Police.

WHERE TO EAT AND DRINK ⓘ

If you're in Rochford on a Sunday, try the freshly caught cockles and seafood from the stall beside the New Ship Inn in the town centre or try an 'eat-as-much-as-you-like' Indian meal at the **Taste of Raj** directly opposite. Other watering holes in the town include the **Kings Head Inn** in Market Square and the **Antique Tea Rooms** in South Street.

---

③ Follow the waymark through the kissing gate and join the river bank path. With the river mudflats and salt marsh on your right, continue ahead along the grassy sea wall. Look left to see the distinctive Saxon tower of the church at Great Stambridge. Continue around the peninsula of **Bartonhall Creek**, a popular feasting ground of mudflats for migrating birds. As you reach the north western tip, walk left down the embankment to the fingerpost, leaving the **Roach Valley Way**, and turn left towards **Great Stambridge** to pass a number of old Essex barns converted into modern housing. Maintain direction along the field-edge path towards houses and after ½ mile (800m) the path passes Ash Tree Court and emerges on the **Stambridge Road**. Turn right into Great Stambridge past the Royal Oak pub and notice the array of attractive Victorian villas and the post office.

WHAT TO LOOK FOR ⓘ

Visit **St Mary and All Saints Church** at Stambridge with its distinctive square Saxon tower and look for the stained-glass memorial window known as the Winthrop Window. It was placed in the church by the American descendants of Stambridge's most famous resident, John Winthrop who, in 1630, set sail for the Americas in the *Arabella* and went on to become the first Governor of Boston.

---

④ Just before the post office, turn left into **Stewards Elm Farm Lane** and follow the waymark over the footbridge. Maintain direction between a series of paddocks until you reach the kissing gate and turn left to follow the field-edge path keeping **Ragstone Lodge** and the **Rectory** on your left. Continue on the cross-field path following the waymarks right, left, then half right past houses on your right, until you meet **Stambridge Road**.

⑤ Turn right at the **Cherry Tree** public house and after about 200yds (183m), turn left into **Mill Lane**, then right on to the cross-field path to join **Rocheway** past the houses into **East Street** and pass the New Ship Inn on your right. Turn left into **South Street** and return to the car park.

WHILE YOU'RE THERE ⓘ

Continuing the theme of peculiarity in Rochford don't forget to visit **St Andrew's Church**, the only church in England which stands in the middle of a golf course. Just opposite is **Rochford Hall**, part residential and part home of the Rochford Hundred Golf Club. The hall stands on the site of the residence of Sir Thomas Boleyn whose daughter, Anne, married Henry VIII in 1533. She was executed three years later, but not before she had given birth to a son, who died, and a daughter who went on to become Queen Elizabeth I.

Roaming Around Hanningfield Reservoir

Birds, wildlife, and a nature walk through meadows and woodlands.

•DISTANCE•	3½ miles (5.7km)
•MINIMUM TIME•	1hr 30min
•ASCENT / GRADIENT•	Negligible
•LEVEL OF DIFFICULTY•	
•PATHS•	Grassy and gravel forest tracks, prone to mud after rains, some boardwalk
•LANDSCAPE•	Reservoir, forest and grassy meadow
•SUGGESTED MAP•	aqua3 OS Explorer 175 Southend-on-Sea & Basildon
•START / FINISH•	Grid reference: TQ 725971
•DOG FRIENDLINESS•	No-go area except for guide dogs
•PARKING•	Free parking at the Visitor Centre, Hawkswood Road entrance. Gates close at 5PM
•PUBLIC TOILETS•	Visitor Centre

BACKGROUND TO THE WALK

If you're a birdwatcher, or just enjoy nature, then Hanningfield Reservoir and Nature Reserve is the place for you. The south eastern shores of the 970 acre (393ha) reservoir have been set aside as a nature reserve by the Essex Water Company and are a Site of Special Scientific Interest (SSSI). Managed by the Essex Wildlife Trust, it is best known for the prolific numbers of wintering and breeding wildfowl. Among them are nationally important numbers of coot, gadwall and tufted duck. If you're there in early winter you will also see pintails in large numbers. The chalk-based sludge on the western side of the reservoir supports plants uncommon in Essex, such as golden dock and marsh dock.

Pleasant Strolling

An interesting nature trail leads through the woodland, where there are several especially well-constructed bird hides overlooking the reservoir and banks enabling you to spend all day spotting species such as pochard, shoveler, shelduck and great crested grebe. But for non-twitchers, waymarked trails lead through ancient coppice and secondary woodland, with ponds, hedges and ditches. Pleasant strolls through four different woods, Chestnut, Peninsular, Well Wood and Hawkswood are there to be enjoyed.

Coppiced Woodland

Hanningfield Reservoir was built to provide water for an increased population after World War Two and, in the 1960s, the area which forms part of today's nature reserve, was planted with conifers. Thirty years later, in 1992, the Essex Wildlife Trust took over management of the site and the reserve is, today, renowned for its abundant wildlife. In Chestnut Wood there are areas of Scots pine which have been thinned to allow in light to the cleared sunny grasslands, which are an excellent habitat for butterflies and crickets. Ponds, ditches and piles of dead wood have attracted dragonflies, newts and grass snakes. In Peninsular Wood, near Point and Oak Hides, warblers nest and feed in an area which was cleared and allowed to regenerate as scrub. And in Well Wood and Hawkswood you can see the perimeters of ancient woodlands where coppiced hornbeams and hazel allow the old plant and animal communities to flourish once more.

Spend some time in the Visitor Centre, either before or after your nature walk, to see some novel conservation ideas in action, such as composting toilets which need no flush and a log-burning stove using wood from the reserve. Water is conserved by collecting rain water from a large roof and using it to top up two wildlife ponds beside the Visitor Centre. You can use complimentary binoculars (donation appreciated) to spot dozens of birds feeding at one of these ponds from the viewing gallery inside the centre.

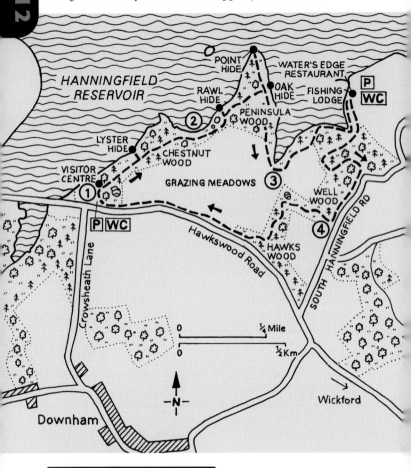

Walk 12 Directions

① From the **Visitor Centre**, take the path to **waymark C1** and detour left for views of the reservoir from **Lyster Hide**. Return to **C1** and continue along the path through **Chestnut Wood** for 100yds (91m). At **waymark C2**, bear right towards the clearing and then go straight ahead towards tall oaks and **waymark C4**. Bear right here, over the wooden footbridge, passing the pond on your left, and continue until you reach **waymark C5** on the

WALK 12

edge of the wood. Ahead are grazing meadows. Turn left along the gravel path, keeping the meadow on your right, and follow the boardwalk to a clearing with deep water ponds and seating made from split trunks.

② Walk left past **waymark 7** to **Rawl Hide**, for good views of the reservoir and the reed covered embankment on the left. Now return to **waymark 7**, turn left on to the wide grassy path to enter **Peninsular Wood** and continue to **waymark 6**. Bear half left for 100yds (91m) and pass by Oak Hide to maintain direction to the tip of the peninsula and **waymark 5**, where you'll find **Point Hide**. Retrace your steps to **waymark 4** and walk ahead with the reservoir on your left. Maintain direction through thick forest passing **waymarks 3** and **2**, where you turn left and cross the bridge over the ditch.

③ Ignore the stile across to Hawkswood and turn left through thick forest for 200yds (183m) to **waymark B** and enter **Well Wood**. Turn left and then right for 200yds (183m) until you meet **waymark A**, with the **Fishing Lodge** and **Water's Edge** off to the left. Swing right and

walk straight ahead, between coppiced trees with the high embankment on your left denoting the old boundary of the woods, to **waymark C**. Turn left, keeping meadows on your right, to **waymark D**. Turn left to **waymark K** and right to **waymark H**. Turn right again, into an area of less dense woodland with South Hanningfield Road on your left.

④ At **waymark F,** continue along the wide bridleway to a clearing of coppiced hornbeams. Descend timber steps, and past several small ponds to **waymark E** to enter **Hawkswood** passing **waymarks H1, H2** and **H3** in quick succession. At H3 bear right over an earth bridge to **H10**, with meadow on your right, and bear left towards **H9** and **H11**. From here the path leads straight through hedgerows and a double set of kissing gates. Notice the pond on your right surrounded by a circle of chestnut trees and return to the car park.

Walk 13

Places and Palaces in Danbury Country Park

A gentle countryside walk, with panoramic views, exploring ancient woodland, flower-filled meadows and bird-filled lakes.

•DISTANCE•	4 miles (6.4km)
•MINIMUM TIME•	2hrs
•ASCENT / GRADIENT•	164ft (50m)
•LEVEL OF DIFFICULTY•	🚶 🚶 🚶
•PATHS•	Grass and woodland paths, field paths, some road
•LANDSCAPE•	Ancient woodland, lakes, meadows
•SUGGESTED MAP•	aqua3 OS Explorer 183 Chelmsford & The Rodings, Maldon & Witham
•START / FINISH•	Grid reference: TL 781050
•DOG FRIENDLINESS•	Some open space but must be on lead most of way
•PARKING•	Free car park off Main Road opposite library and inside Danbury Country Park
•PUBLIC TOILETS•	Main Road car park, car parks at Danbury Country Park which also have facilities for disabled

BACKGROUND TO THE WALK

Danbury is surrounded by delightful woodland, much of it common land, and is the largest area of woodland in Essex after Epping Forest. Steep hillocks and heathland soil have prevented intensive arable farming and, as a result, its environs are now designated nature reserves, owned and managed by various conservation agencies, including the National Trust and the Essex Wildlife Trust. These areas pack in a huge variety of habitats in a relatively small space and, if you're a lover of woodland walks, then a stroll around Danbury is bound to appeal.

Diminutive Danbury
The village is perched on a hill, 350ft (107m) above sea level, on the A414 east of Chemsford. The slender spire of St John the Baptist Church is visible for miles around, especially if you're approaching along the A12 from London. This superb setting compensates for what Danbury lacks in historic buildings and, apart from the church, there is little to detain you in the village.

From Place to Palace
On this gentle walk you'll discover some characterful 18th- and 19th-century farms and cottages and the rather splendid 16th-century Danbury Palace, (off limits to the public) inside the country park. Sir Walter Mildmay, founder of Emmanuel College, Cambridge, built the house you see today and called it Danbury Place. But when it was sold to the Church of England in 1845 for £24,700, and occupied by George Murray, 96th Bishop of Rochester, it became known as Danbury Palace, reflecting its change in status.

In the 13th century, aristocratic families went deer hunting in the park, which had been a gift to Geoffrey de Mandeville, 1st Earl of Essex, by William I. Today the country park has three delightful duck-filled lakes, picnic areas and impressive specimens of beech and oak. Beside the palace there are beautiful ornamental gardens filled, in summer, with flowers from Asia and the Americas, while herbaceous perennials attract a host of butterflies.

Your journey's end is at St John the Baptist Church, in a location where Iron Age farmers once lived. Having risen to these comparatively dizzy heights, look southwards where the views are both impressive and extensive, and you soon understand why the Saxons fortified this position. The Normans, following in their footsteps, built the church and everyone was happy for a time. But, when Henry VIII decreed that the monasteries should be dissolved in 1536, church furnishings throughout the land were sold to avoid confiscation. The story goes that an enterprising medieval DIY enthusiast used much of the wood from the church to kit out the Griffin Inn across the road and, until a few decades ago, part of the rood screen could still be seen above the bar.

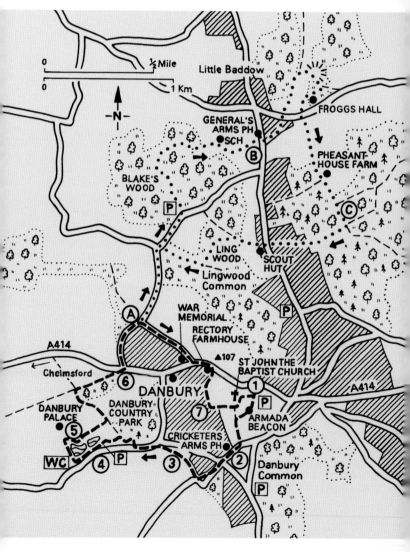

Walk 13

Walk 13 Directions

① Leave the car park via the grassy path to the right of the leisure centre. Walk downhill, with the playing fields left and hedgerows right. One hundred yards (91m) after the **Armada beacon**, turn left at the cross path for panoramic views of south Essex towards Kent.

② Turn right into **Pennyroyal Road** past the Cricketers Arms, then cross **Bicknacre Road** into **Sporehams Lane**. Follow the path marked 'Butts Green'. At a signpost, take a track through dwarf oaks and gorse, to cross a bridge. After 25yds (23m), turn right, past houses in **Fitzwalter Lane**.

③ At the last house, called **Dane View**, keep left and follow the footpath through woodland to **Woodhill Road**, and turn left to the sign marking the entrance to **Danbury Country Park** on the right. In the car park take the kissing gate on the left and go left again on to the path just before the information board.

④ Maintain direction past another car park and a second lake, until you reach the toilets. Turn right between the lakes, and continue ahead to reach the red brick perimeter wall of the **Danbury Conference Centre and Palace**.

⑤ Turn right through formal gardens and, with the lake on your right, follow the path half left through woods. Maintain direction uphill, diagonally across a meadow and through the kissing gate. From the kissing gate, walk half left uphill towards the copse. Follow the boardwalk around the small water-filled gravel pit, then take the path uphill between red-and-white painted posts and continue ahead, passing a yellow waymark. Cross the meadow towards the oak trees, keeping the white metal posts to your right.

> **WHERE TO EAT AND DRINK**
> The **Cricketers Arms** makes a good stop for liquid refreshment and also serves a range of bar meals. Try the **Griffin Inn**, just across the road from the church, for great snacks and sandwiches.

⑥ At the last white post, turn left and cross the stile carefully on to the busy **A414**. Cross the road into **Riffhams Lane**, and walk uphill to **Elm Green Lane**. Here turn right, uphill, to the **A414** by the war memorial on the green. Cross the A414, turn left along the verge and right along the footpath beside the **Rectory Farmhouse**.

⑦ At the T-junction turn left for views of St John the Baptist Church and graveyards. At the second T-junction, turn left to visit the church. Turn right to rejoin your outward path past the radio mast and return to the car park.

> **WHAT TO LOOK FOR**
> St John the Baptist Church is famous for its oak carvings of three knights; one drawing his sword, another sheathing his sword and a third in prayer. In 1779 grave-diggers hit upon a lead coffin beside one of the carvings, only to discover the body of one of these knights, preserved in formaldehyde.

> **WHILE YOU'RE THERE**
> Visit Danbury Palace's 18th-century **Ice House**. Ice was collected from lakes, or imported from Scandinavia and America, and stored here between layers of straw. It was then cut up and popped into summer drinks and desserts.

Danbury Wildlife

A longer loop to encompass the woods and wildlife around Danbury.
See map and information panel for Walk 13

•DISTANCE•	5½ miles (8.8km)
•MINIMUM TIME•	2hrs 30min
•ASCENT / GRADIENT•	148ft (45m) ▲▲ ▲▲ ▲
•LEVEL OF DIFFICULTY•	🚶 🚶 🚶

Walk 14 Directions (Walk 13 option)

From Point **Ⓐ** continue along **Riffhams Lane** and, at the junction, bear right into **Riffhams Chase** and left into **Blakes Wood** car park. Take the path to the left of the information board, into a dense area of Blakes Wood dominated by hornbeam and chestnut, and which in spring comes alive with impressive displays of bluebells. Keep the stream to your left and note the many varieties of fungi sprouting on fallen timber.

After 300yds (274m) you reach an area of fallen trees, the result of storm damage in 1987, which the Essex Wildlife Trust have fenced off as an experiment to allow natural regeneration. The path now rises leaving the stream behind, and you emerge into **Colam Lane** passing the school on your left. Follow the footpath into **Parsonage Lane** to meet **The Ridge** with the General's Arms pub on the left, Point **Ⓑ**.

At **Parsonage Lane** turn right and take the first left into **Mill Lane**. Cross **Spring Elms Lane** and follow the footpath, keeping the white house on your right. Pass the sign

for **Heather Hills Nature Reserve** and, at the next fingerpost, turn right past viewpoints across farmland to your left. At the next fingerpost turn right, passing the brick walls enclosing **Froggs Hall** on your left. Cross a stile, turn immediately left through woodland and, after 200yds (183m), cross **Spring Elms Lane** to pick up the footpath to a bridleway, **Postman's Lane**. Keep the grazing land of Pheasanthouse Farm on your left.

You are now deep in the heart of the **Danbury Ridge**, a 240 acre (97ha) area of long established woodlands. Here you may see green woodpeckers or spot butterflies hovering on hemp agrimony. At an information board, Point **Ⓒ**, turn right into the residential area of **Fir Tree Lane**, cross **The Ridge** and pick up the footpath to the right of the bus stop. Pass the scout hut on your left, and cross the stile into **Lingwood**. Turn right at the cross path where a bench gives fine views of Danbury village. Lingwood used to be grazing land but is now covered with birch and oak where the National Trust has maintained clearings to retain birds, insects and plants in their natural habitats. The path continues to **Riffhams Chase** where you turn left into **Riffhams Lane** to rejoin Walk 13.

Chelmsford City Walk

An easy ramble highlighting some historic buildings.

·DISTANCE·	3 miles (4.8km)
·MINIMUM TIME·	1hr 15min
·ASCENT / GRADIENT·	Negligible
·LEVEL OF DIFFICULTY·	
·PATHS·	Pedestrianised streets and pavements
·LANDSCAPE·	Historic streets and buildings
·SUGGESTED MAP·	aqua3 OS Explorer 183 Chelmsford & The Rodings, Maldon & Witham
·START / FINISH·	Grid reference: TL 713067
·DOG FRIENDLINESS·	Pedestrianised areas provide traffic-free walking but dogs aren't allowed in shops and restaurants
·PARKING·	Numerous pay-and-display car parks in city centre
·PUBLIC TOILETS·	Duke Street

Walk 15 **Directions**

Once a small Roman military settlement located on slightly raised ground near the junction of the River Cam and the River Chelmer, Chelmsford was known as *Caesaromagus* or Caesar's Plain, and was the only place name in Roman Britain to have an imperial prefix. Granted a market charter in 1218, it became the county town of Essex, a position it still holds today.

From **Bond Street car park**, join the **High Street** to **Shire Hall**, site of the assizes and quarter sessions where, 350 years ago, Nonconformists and witches were tried in open court beneath a timber-framed canopy. Today the 18th-century building is used as the Magistrates Court.

Turn left at **Shire Hall** and take the first turning on the right to England's smallest cathedral. In the grounds, look for the triangular gravestone dedicated to three Marys, Mary Ann Wolmar, Mary Elizabeth Eve and Mary Smith, who perished in a fire which partially destroyed the town in 1808. Note the grim epitaph 'Prepare for death ere ye retire to rest, for ye know not what a day may bring forth'. Parts of the cathedral date back to 1420; on the south east side is a figure of St Peter holding a Yale key. Walk clockwise around the cathedral passing old sunken gravestones and leave the grounds the same way you came in.

Cross **Tindal Square** passing the statue of 19th-century judge, Chief Justice Nicholas Tindal, who was

WHILE YOU'RE THERE
Two free museums, right next door to each other and a short walk from the town centre, in Oakland Park, are the **Chelmsford and Essex Museum**, for displays of local and social history and the **Essex Regiment Museum** for military exhibits and a large archive of photographs, letters and diaries.

WHAT TO LOOK FOR ℹ️

Look for the blue plaques, commemorating famous people, on buildings around the town. They include Thomas Hooker, the founder of Connecticut in 1636, and others who helped shape Chelmsford's history, such as Guglielmo Marconi, 'the Father of Wireless' who established the world's first radio factory in New Street.

born and bred in Chelmsford. Walk along **Tindal Street** passing Judge Tindal's Tavern on the left, to the traffic lights at **New London Road**. Here, turn right and cross the bridge over the River Cam to **Parkway**. Just around the corner, beside the subway, an information panel describes the site of a 13th-century Dominican friary. Take the subway and follow the signs for the **C & E Hospital**. As you emerge you see the yellow brick Infirmary and Dispensary on your right.

Continue past the hospital to where a pathway to the right leads to a statue of Graham Gooch, captain of Essex and England cricket teams. Just past the statue, and along a pathway parallel with **New London Road**, are two Victorian villas, Thornwood and Bellefield. The first mayor of Chelmsford, Frederick Chancellor lived at Bellefield until his death in 1918.

Continue along New London Road for more examples of fine

WHERE TO EAT AND DRINK ℹ️

There's a wide choice of restaurants, cafés and atmospheric pubs along this route including the delightful Bay Horse pub, a weather-boarded 17th-century inn with a peg tile roof in Moulsham Street, and a number of riverside pavement-style coffee shops including Costa Café next to the Meadway shopping centre.

Victorian-style houses and attractive terraced cottages, many of which have been converted into offices. A little further up on the left is the delightful Melford Villas, now given over to bed and breakfast accomodation. Immediately next door is the street's oldest business, Lucking & Sons, funeral directors, which is adjacent to the overgrown Nonconformists' cemetery. Here is the grave of an escaped slave who made it all the way to Chelmsford from New Orleans.

Turn left into **Elm Road** and left again into **Moulsham Street**, the site of the old London Road and the former manor of Moulsham, given to Thomas Mildmay by Henry VIII for his role as receiver of monies during the dissolution of the monasteries. The street contains many listed buildings, including six almhouses founded by Thomas Mildmay, and rebuilt in 1758. Further along there are shops and cottages where the upper storeys overhang. A particularly good example is No 41,which dates back to the 15th century.

At the end of **Moulsham Street**, cross **Parkway** via the subway to reach the High Street. Just after **Baddow Street**, on the right, is the former Regent Playhouse Theatre, now a trendy café. On **Springfield Road**, the next turning on the right, is the site of the Black Boy Inn, immortalised by Charles Dickens in *The Pickwick Papers*.

Back in the **High Street**, on the right, is the Royal Bank of Scotland, the former Mansion House and lodgings of the judge when he came to sit at the assizes. **Shire Hall** is straight ahead and from here you return to the car park.

Walk 16

Along the River Valley to Earls Colne

A fairly challenging walk along a disused railway track, now a nature reserve, and through ancient woodland.

•DISTANCE•	6½ miles (10.4km)
•MINIMUM TIME•	3hrs 30min
•ASCENT / GRADIENT•	78ft (24m) ▲▲▲
•LEVEL OF DIFFICULTY•	🚶🚶 🚶🚶 🚶🚶
•PATHS•	Grassy with some muddy tracks, forest and field-edge paths, 3 stiles
•LANDSCAPE•	Disused railway line, ancient woodland, riverside and grazing meadows
•SUGGESTED MAP•	aqua3 OS Explorer 195 Braintree & Saffron Walden
•START / FINISH•	Grid reference: TL 855290
•DOG FRIENDLINESS•	Some stiles only suitable for chihuahuas, bigger dogs will need to be lifted
•PARKING•	Free parking at Queens Road car park in Earls Colne
•PUBLIC TOILETS•	Queens Road car park

BACKGROUND TO THE WALK

Is this the loveliest valley in all Essex? Judge for yourself as you follow the meandering River Colne and visit the delightful village of Earls Colne where the de Vere family, Earls of Oxford and one of the greatest families in English history, left their name. Here you will find a lovely view from the split-timber seating beside St Andrew's Church, with its tower visible for miles around; a nature reserve along a disused railway track, which has been cut back allowing wildlife to flourish, and the ancient woodlands of Chalkney Woods.

A Disused Railway Line

The Colne Valley Railway opened in 1860 and soon brought prosperity to the valley. Earls Colne, one of the stations on the line, was built by the Hunt family who developed the Atlas Works, which produced farming equipment until it closed in 1988. The line was used to import raw materials and to despatch the finished product, but since its closure in 1965 the track side vegetation has become a rich habitat for wildlife, with plenty of trees and shrubs providing heavy shade. As you walk along the disused track you will see evidence of coppicing which allows light to reach the ground, which in turn allows wildlife such as butterflies and other insects to proliferate.

Chalkney Wood dates back to 1605 when it was owned by the de Vere family. This walk takes you through the woods where conifers are gradually being replaced with traditional species to regenerate the woodland. You'll also see, near the kennels, an 18th-century watermill which last worked in the 1930s and is now a private residence. In the Alder Valley are the remains of conifer plantations established in the 1960s, but today the area supports more moss and liverworts than any other wood in East Anglia. You'll also pass close to the Wool Track, believed to be an ancient Roman road linking Colchester and Cambridge, and

Walk 16

come across a prominent bank which enclosed the woods as a swine park where pigs would feed on acorns amongst the coppice.

Brickfields and Long Meadow Nature Reserve, bordered by woodland of oak, ash and hawthorn, has plenty of boggy areas and wet grassland. It is small, but has plenty of insect life. The ponds, surrounded by acacia and rhododendron, are home to newts, frogs and dragonflies. A major feature of the area is the anthills, which house huge colonies of yellow ants. Long Meadow, used for grazing, is free of fertilisers and pesticides, and as a result supports plenty of wildlife and a variety of grasses such as yarrow and birds trefoil. Near by you should also find a rare surviving elm tree.

Walk 16 **Directions**

① From the car park, turn left and left again into **Burrows Road**. Cross **Hilly Bunnies Road** and maintain direction to the **Wildside waymark**. Here bear slightly right, then left on to the cross-field path, downhill

across the golf course. Cross the footbridge following the yellow waymark over the **River Colne**. Follow the path for 70yds (64m) and bear left on the lesser path towards trees to the waymarked stile and information board marking the entrance to the railway nature reserve. Turn right on to the

Walk 16

railway embankment and maintain direction keeping the river and golf course on your right. Cross the footbridge over the **River Peb** and maintain your direction for about 600yds (549m).

② Leave the reserve by turning right at a collection of waymarks. Keep the fence of the sewage works on your left and follow the grassy path to reach **Colne Ford Road**. Turn left, cross the road, and follow the footpath and waymark between house Nos 20 and 22 through the wooden gate. Maintain direction across the meadow with the **River Colne** down on your right until you climb stile No 2.

WHERE TO EAT AND DRINK i
A good selection of eateries can be found in the High Street. Choose from the **Colne Valley Tandoori** restaurant which serves an 'eat-as-much-as-you-like' buffet on Sunday evenings or relax with your tired dog in the garden of the **Castle** pub. In Colneford Road you can enjoy a meal and drink at the **Platypus Creek** restaurant by the River Colne.

③ Turn right and cross the bridge over the Colne, passing kennels and **Chalkney Mill** on your right, and maintain direction into **Chalkney Wood**. Walk for 300yds (274m), take the second path on your right and go along the straight bridleway, bounded on the left by Corsican pine. Maintain direction for 500yds (457m) and bear right to the parking area. Take the wide downhill track for 300yds (274m) and turn left into **Tey Road** at **Peek's Corner**.

④ After 300yds (274m) turn right at the fingerpost and go along the field-edge path keeping the hedgerows on your right. Cross the

WHAT TO LOOK FOR i
The de Veres were great crusaders and were associated with a legendary silver star which was won outside the walls of Antioch on their first crusade. The family left their mark in the form of a star on buildings in this area of Essex, leaving no one in any doubt as to who owned and constructed them. One of these buildings is the unique star-studded tower of **St Andrew's Church**.

earth bridge through trees, maintain direction uphill, and pass Tilekiln Farm, on your right, to **Coggeshall Road**.

⑤ Turn right at Coggeshall Road and after 200yds (183m) turn left at the fingerpost marked **Park Lane**. Follow the path through the kissing gate and turn immediately right along the path bounded by thick gorse bushes. Follow the path left and downhill, keeping woods on your right, until you reach the **Wildside** waymarked stile. Cross the stile and walk along the field-edge path, keeping the hedgerow on your right, to an earth bridge where you turn right over the stream.

⑥ Take the path past a Brickfields information board on your right and turn right into **Park Lane** with St Andrews Church on your left. Turn left into **Coggeshall Road** and the **High Street** and return to the car park.

WHILE YOU'RE THERE
If you're driving, head up to the **East Anglian Railway Museum** at Chappel Station to view a fine collection of goods and passenger rolling stock. Railway enthusiasts and children alike will love the interactive signal boxes and video displays in this working museum which covers a century of railway engineering in East Anglia.

Six Farms and a Castle at Hedingham

Explore the wealth of history packed into this tiny area.

•DISTANCE•	3½ miles (5.7km)
•MINIMUM TIME•	1hr 30min
•ASCENT / GRADIENT•	64ft (20m)
•LEVEL OF DIFFICULTY•	
•PATHS•	Grassy, field-edge and farm tracks, some woodland and town streets
•LANDSCAPE•	Arable and grazing farmland, patches of woodland
•SUGGESTED MAP•	aqua3 OS Explorer 195 Braintree & Saffron Walden
•START / FINISH•	Grid reference: TL 784356
•DOG FRIENDLINESS•	On lead round farms and on country lanes. Lots of other dogs around
•PARKING•	Informal street parking in Castle Hedingham village
•PUBLIC TOILETS•	Behind Castle Hedingham Club in Church Lane

BACKGROUND TO THE WALK

The Castle Hedingham story begins with Aubrey de Vere, a favourite knight of William the Conqueror, who was rewarded for his valour at the Battle of Hastings with land, which included Kensington and Earls Court in London. Aubrey's son built Castle Hedingham in 1140, which became the de Vere stronghold for the next 550 years and is still owned today by one of their descendants.

The de Veres became extremely rich and influential over the years and often entertained royalty, including Henry VIII and Elizabeth I. But they are best known for being great crusaders, fighting alongside Richard I (Richard the Lionheart) and taking leading parts in the famous battles at Crecy, Poitiers, Agincourt and Bosworth. Robert de Vere, 3rd Earl of Oxford, was one of the barons who persuaded King John to sign the Magna Carta at Runnymede in 1215.

But in 1703 the de Vere title fell out of use when Aubrey, 20th Earl of Oxford died, leaving no sons. The castle was bought by Sir William Ashhurst, MP and Lord Mayor of London, who landscaped the grounds and built a fine country house, which was completed in 1719. The estate eventually passed to his great grandaughter, Elizabeth Houghton, who married Lewis Majendie. The Majendies owned Hedingham for 250 years before it was inherited by a cousin who was descended from the de Veres.

A Star and Boar

This walk starts from the grand Norman Church of St Nicholas where, above the window of the Tudor bell tower, you can see the star and the boar, both symbols of the de Vere family. The star is said to have fallen from heaven upon the shield of the first de Vere on one of the crusades and since then has become the family emblem. The castle dominates the view as you walk along Castle Lane and uphill into open countryside dotted with farms, which date from the 16th and 17th centuries, and arable and grazing land.

Walk 17

Distinguished Drinkers

The tranquillity of the surrounding countryside is a far cry from the mayhem of the crusades and other famous battles. When you return to the village via a pleasant country lane, you cannot fail to notice the castle looming in the distance, a constant reminder of the power and influence of the de Vere dynasty. Back in the village, the tiny houses in Church Ponds cluster around the church, while those in Church Lane were the homes of weavers, built 400 years ago when the community benefited from the wool industry. Wander around and perhaps call in at the oldest pub, the Bell Inn, which dates back 500 years and is where Disraeli downed a pint or two after a speech. Or relax at the bar which, it is said, supported one or two de Veres too.

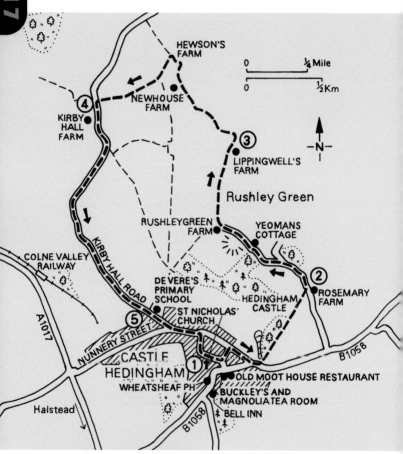

Walk 17 Directions

① With the church on your right, walk along **Church Ponds** into **Falcon Square** with its medieval houses. Turn left into **Castle Lane** with the 17th-century Youth Hostel

building on your right and walk uphill to **Bayley Street**. Cross the road and, at the castle entrance, turn right and walk to the T-junction. Turn left into **Sudbury Road** and, just after **New Park Road** on your right, turn left at the narrow track to **Rosemary's Farm**.

Walk 17

WHILE YOU'RE THERE ⓘ

Moorhens, herons, kingfishers and woodpeckers can be seen at the farm park of the **Colne Valley Railway**. Enjoy a half-day exploring the working steam railway at this family attraction and maybe try the goodies served in the buffet carriage at this delightful country railway station before, or after a visit, to **Castle Hedingham** with its Banqueting Hall and Minstrels' Gallery.

② Turn left, follow the track to the Y-junction and bear left passing the red brick, thatched Keepers Cottage on your left. Pass several houses and admire the fine view of rolling countryside beyond the stile on your left, opposite **Yeoman's Cottage**. After 200yds (183m) the track bears right with the converted barns of **Rushleygreen Farm** on your left. Ignore the timber footbridge immediately after the farm and continue along the main farm track with arable fields away to your left.

③ Pass **Lippingwell's Farm** on your right, bear left across the meandering field-edge path passing the front of **Newhouse Farm**, with its pond on your left, and continue to **Hewson's Farm** and the brick-built tower on your right. Turn sharp left at the fingerpost along the field-edge path to the small row of trees at the rear of **Newhouse Farm**.

At the waymark bear right across another field-edge path to **Kirby Hall Farm**.

④ Turn left at the crossroads to **Kirby Hall Road** and, ignoring all footpaths left and right, follow this wide farm track passing hedgerows and rows of trees to return to **Castle Hedingham**. On the way, pass through high embankments of hedgerows and an impressive row of oak trees. Before rising towards the village of Hedingham you can see the top of the castle keep, peering above trees to your half left.

⑤ Walking into the village, pass de Vere's Primary School and the modern housing estate on your left. At the T-junction, turn left into **Nunnery Street** and right into **Crown Street**, where jettied buildings and medieval cottages herald your return to the old village and the church.

WHAT TO LOOK FOR ⓘ

Explore the lane leading down to the old school house from the police station in Queen Street. This is where the **de Vere Silk Weavers** manufactured the silk for the wedding dresses for the late Diana, Princess of Wales and the present Duchess of York. If you have time, visit the interior of **St Nicholas' Church** where the de Vere star and boar can be seen in the nave roof.

WHERE TO EAT AND DRINK ⓘ

A good choice of old pubs, restaurants and tea rooms are clustered in and around St James Street. For atmosphere and fine food try the 15th-century **Old Moot House**. Tea and tasty cakes can be enjoyed at the delightful **Buckleys & The Magnolia Tea Room** just along the street. The 18th-century **Wheatsheaf** in Queen Street has a dog-friendly garden at the rear and does children's meals.

Walk 18

Halstead's Courtaulds Connection

A charming town and country walk discovering the influence of the Courtauld family and their textile legacy.

•DISTANCE•	3 miles (4.8km)
•MINIMUM TIME•	1hr 15min
•ASCENT / GRADIENT•	90ft (27m) ▲ ▲ ▲
•LEVEL OF DIFFICULTY•	🕴 🕴🕴 🕴🕴
•PATHS•	Town streets and grassy tracks
•LANDSCAPE•	Urban, river and meadow
•SUGGESTED MAP•	aqua3 OS Explorer 195 Braintree & Saffron Walden
•START / FINISH•	Grid reference: TL 812306
•DOG FRIENDLINESS•	Pleasant on-lead town walk but most dogs will prefer the meadow
•PARKING•	Pay-and-display in Chapel Street and Mill Bridge
•PUBLIC TOILETS•	Chapel Street

BACKGROUND TO THE WALK

Surrounded by the gentle rolling countryside of the Colne Valley in north Essex, Halstead developed over many centuries as a busy market town and, in the Middle Ages, much of its prosperity came from the wool trade. In the early 19th century Samuel Courtauld (1793–1881), an industrious and successful businessman, brought a new lease of life to the town. A descendant of a Huguenot refugee family, he set up in business as a silk throwster (a person who twists silk fibres into thread) and his family went on to found the internationally known Courtaulds company.

A Royal Trendsetter

Courtaulds had its share of ups and downs, but always seemed one step ahead of its competitors, due to a policy of diversification. When the silk industry dwindled, mainly due to French competition, the company specialised in the production of mourning crêpe, which was to become the definitive fashion material during, and after, Queen Victoria's reign (1837–1901). When crêpe fell out of favour, Courtaulds turned to the manufacture of artificial silk which became such a success that brand name materials such as Celanese saw the company through the depression of the 1930s.

The Courtaulds connection with Halstead began in 1825 when Samuel Courtauld bought the present Townsford Mill and converted it to produce silk-woven fabrics; much of the raw material was imported in bulk from India. In those days the cloth was produced in the workers' homes and some of these early weavers' cottages can still be seen next to the mill in Bridge Street. By 1891 the mill became one of England's largest employers, where 1,400 people, the vast majority young girls and women, toiled at 1,000 looms.

The Courtauld family left legacies throughout Halstead and on this walk you will discover some of them, such as the Jubilee Fountain at the top of Market Street, on a spot previously occupied by the old Market Cross. In Hedingham Lane you can see the

Courtaulds workers' houses which are named after characters and titles from Jane Austen's novels. The family also footed the bill for building Halstead Cottage Hospital while the Homes of Rest next door, a semi-circular row of single-storey dwellings built in 1923, provided much-needed housing for retired silk weavers.

Courtauld Institute

Samuel Courtauld became very rich, and lived to the ripe old age of 88 in an impressive Tudor mansion called Gosfield Hall, a few miles from Halstead. During the 1920s his great-nephew and namesake would often drive or walk along Box Mill where he apparently took a dislike to the housing and duly replaced them with his own preferred style of cottages. The young Samuel (1876–1947) went on to establish the Courtauld Institute of Art in London before he died. In 1982 Courtaulds factory finally closed down but there's little doubt that this name lives on in Halstead.

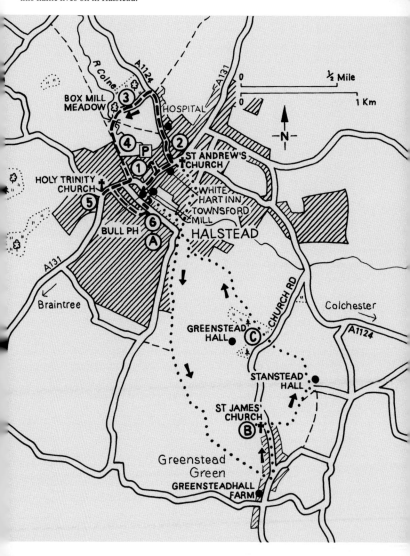

Walk 18

Walk 18 Directions

① Turn right into **Chapel Street** then left into the **High Street** by the post office. Walk up **Market Hill** to the **Jubilee Fountain** for panoramic views of the layout of the town and note the distant Mount Hill, proof that not all of Essex is flat.

② Turn left into **Hedingham Road** (A1124) passing Halstead Hospital and the Courtauld Homes of Rest on your right. Turn left into **Box Mill Lane** where several cottages and larger dwellings attest to further building by the Courtaulds.

WHAT TO LOOK FOR

Three-storeyed weavers' homes were still fairly common in Halstead during the 19th and early 20th centuries. Some of these survive in **Weavers Row** near Parsonage Street. The upper and lower floors were used as domestic quarters while the middle floor, which had one room extending the length of the row, was used as a weaving workshop.

---

③ At the end of Box Mill Lane, maintain direction into **Box Mill Meadow**, a fine picnic spot, and cross the footbridge over the **River Colne** as it flows south into the town. Along the river bank, traces of rubble are all that remain of the two mills, one a watermill and the other wind powered, that once occupied this spot. Take the footpath to the left.

WHILE YOU'RE THERE

Some of the oldest houses in Halstead, dating back to the 14th century, can be seen at the bottom of Chapel Hill. At the top of the High Street is the flint and rubble **St Andrew's Church** with its lovely tower; some parts date back to the 15th century.

---

④ At the edge of **Halstead Town Football Ground**, cross the stile and maintain your direction along the footpath which becomes a grassy track, the former route of the Halstead and Colne Valley Railway. Go straight ahead into **Butler Road**, which was named after R A Butler (1902–82), better known as Rab, Conservative politician and Member of Parliament for Saffron Walden. At the T-junction with **Trinity Street** notice the redevelopment across the road, where flats and a park area called Trinity Court now stand on the site of the old railway station.

⑤ Turn right and walk to **Trinity Church** on your right. Close by are some of the oldest houses in the town. Retrace your steps for a few paces and turn right just after the police station into **New Street**. Note the public gardens opposite the Methodist church, turn left into **Martin Street**, then left again and right into **Factory Lane West** by the tourist information office.

⑥ Turn left into **The Causeway**, Courtaulds old Townsford Mill on the right, and walk ahead into **Bridge Street.** Turn right to cross the bridge over the River Colne and go into the **High Street** to the post office. Pause here awhile to note the varied architecture around you. Walk along **Chapel Street** and return to the car park.

WHERE TO EAT AND DRINK

You are spoilt for choice with a range of tea rooms, restaurants and pubs. Of particular historic interest are two 500-year-old coaching inns in the High Street: the **White Hart** which ran a regular service to Great Yarmouth and the **Bull Hotel,** which featured in the TV series *Lovejoy* starring Ian McShane.

To Greenstead Green

A longer loop walk which takes in a pretty church and rural calm.
See map and information panel for Walk 18

•DISTANCE•	7¾ miles (12.5km)
•MINIMUM TIME•	2hrs 30min
•ASCENT / GRADIENT•	154ft (47m) ▲ ▲ ▲
•LEVEL OF DIFFICULTY•	👫 👫 👫

Walk 19 Directions (Walk 18 option)

To extend the walk to **Greenstead Green** turn right, Point Ⓐ, into **Factory Lane West** passing Townsford Mill at the junction with The Causeway. At the T-junction turn right into **Parsonage Street**, cross the roundabout and take the footpath to the left of **Tiding Hill**, passing behind houses to cross **Highfields** into **South Close.**

Between Nos 20 and 22, take the path towards the meadow and follow the field-edge path south. Maintain direction across the earth bridge and after 500yds (457m) bear left at the fingerpost on the field-edge path. Continue downhill to **Church Road**, turning left at **Greensteadhall Farm** and pass a row of cottages before reaching **St James' Church**, Point Ⓑ.

Greenstead Green owes much of its ecclesiastical heritage to Mary Gee. Born in 1795 she married into an influential Essex family and later became a wealthy widow. She bore the entire cost of constructing St James' Church in 1844, the vicarage and the school, as well as Halstead's Holy Trinity Church.

In St James' look at the north wall which has two plaques, one dedicated to Mary Gee, the other to an American airman whose plane crashed near by in World War Two.

Cross **Church Road** to the fingerpost opposite the vicarage, and take the field-edge path for 250yds (229m) keeping the hedgerow on your right. Turn left, still with the hedgerow on your right, and maintain direction passing **Stanstead Hall**. As you pass a series of paddocks keep to the diverted footpath. Turn left, keeping hedgerows to your left, and follow the path down over the footbridge to **Church Road**, Point Ⓒ.

Pass the Lodge on your right, climb the stile and take the cross-field path diagonally through the meadow. On your left, through trees, is **Greenstead Hall**. Crawl through the next stile and follow the cross-field path diagonally downhill keeping the spire of St Andrew's Church in view in the distance. Follow the path past the rear of houses on your left to join with **Elm Drive** where you turn right into **Balls Chase,** then right again into **Parsonage Street**. Continue uphill to the **High Street** by St Andrew's Church, turn left and return to the car park.

Walk 20

Braintree and the Flitch Way

Braintree's industrial heritage and a stroll along a disused railway line.

•DISTANCE•	5½ miles (8.8km)
•MINIMUM TIME•	2hrs 15min
•ASCENT / GRADIENT•	48ft (15m)
•LEVEL OF DIFFICULTY•	
•PATHS•	Grassy and gravel tracks, some street walking
•LANDSCAPE•	Wildlife-rich railway cuttings, river bank and urban landscape
•SUGGESTED MAP•	aqua3 OS Explorer 195 Braintree & Saffron Walden
•START / FINISH•	Grid reference: TL 760227
•DOG FRIENDLINESS•	Pedestrians and dogs share Flitch Way with cyclists and horses so may have to be on lead
•PARKING•	Pay-and-display at George Yard, Manor Street at rear of library and Braintree Station
•PUBLIC TOILETS•	Braintree Station

Walk 20 Directions

The attractive town sits astride the junction of two Roman roads, where the White Hart Hotel, a former coaching and posting house, now stands. In the 19th century, Samuel Courtauld, a descendant of a Huguenot weaving family, created a successful textile industry in the town; further prosperity was brought by iron foundries and manufacturing businesses including the window-making enterprise set up by Francis Crittall. Crittall started as an ironmonger in the late 19th century and became one of the town's major employers, producing metal-framed windows, the forerunner of double glazing.

In this walk you will discover Courtaulds' and Crittall's contributions to the town and see how Braintree is facing the future with a regeneration programme. Yet for all the changes, the town still retains links with the past with an interesting heritage trail and a linear country park, the Flitch Way, following the railway line, from Braintree to Bishop's Stortford, abandoned in 1969.

Start from **Braintree Station** where a set of buffers terminates the old line from Liverpool Street in London to Bishop's Stortford. Beyond is the **Flitch Way**, a narrow bridleway approached via the path at the western end of the station car park. The Flitch Way crosses the bridge over **Notley Road** and soon becomes a grassy track.

After a mile (1.6 km) the **River Brain** flows under the track. Turn right here over the stile, just before the river, and follow the path past **Clapbridge Farm**, modern housing estates and across meadowland. Keep the river on your right until you reach **Clap Bridge** on **Rayne Road**, the former Roman road of Stane Street. Turn right, continue over the roundabout and into the town to the **White Hart Hotel**.

Walk past the hotel into **Coggeshall Road** to the double roundabout. Cross **Railway Street** and, on your right, there is a block of apartments fronted by a heritage board describing the site of the Crittall's Manor Works, demolished in 1992. Continue along Coggeshall Road and take the first turning left into **John Ray Street**, to a pair of weathered timber gates which mark the entrance to the recreation ground, a gift to the town from Julian Courtauld.

Back in **Coggeshall Road**, turn right into **Cressing Road** to the **Kings Head** pub, where a heritage board describes the site of a grand old oak tree opposite. In 1964 the tree was removed because it was considered too big and dangerous, but many townspeople remember sitting on the bench beneath it to watch the world go by. In Cressing Road there is an interesting mix of late 19th-century cottages, and an impressive thatched row of cottages dating back to 1620.

At the end of Cressing Road cross over to **Clockhouse Way**, a conservation area of houses constructed with concrete blocks, complete with Crittall metal windows. Built for Crittall workers in 1918–19, the design was copied, in 1926, at Silver End (to the

WHERE TO EAT AND DRINK

There are plenty of pubs in Braintree and assorted restaurants, including Indian, Chinese, pizza houses and fish and chip shops. The **White Hart Hotel** opposite Rayne Road (Roman Stane Street) serves excellent bar snacks and wholesome lunches in an atmospheric setting. Try the **Swan** in Bank Street or fill up with a hot breakfast at the café at **Braintree Station** (closed Sunday).

south east of Braintree). Similar, albeit grander, houses can be seen at 146 and 148 Cressing Road.

Return to the junction and continue along **Chapel Hill.** At the end, turn half left to the roundabout then turn right on to **Mill Hill**. Go under the railway bridge, on the left is another heritage board describing the site of an old flour mill which Courtauld converted into a silk mill, and which is now a residential area.

Turn right up **Skitts Lane**, go under the railway bridge and take the first right into **The Yard**, a modern complex of apartments. Keep left and follow the footpath towards the gas works where a heritage board describes the function of Lake and Elliot's Power House, which generated electricity for use by the town's businesses until 1946 when the National Grid started lighting up the country. The firm originally produced cycle parts then expanded into jacks and armour plating for the military. Like other businesses they no longer operate in town, but they have been replaced by new initiatives keeping Braintree the bustling town it has always been. Follow the footpath into **Manor Street**, turn left passing modern developments in Trinovantes Street and return to the car park.

WHILE YOU'RE THERE

Visit the spectacular aisled barns at **Cressing Temple**, built 800 years ago by the warrior monks of the Knights Templar. The Wheat Barn has an interesting exhibition explaining the history of this elite fighting force, whose aim was to protect pilgrims travelling to the Holy Land. If you're there on a Sunday join the free guided tour or wander round the Tudor walled garden.

Walk 21

Langdon – an Old Plot for Eastenders

Explore ancient woodland and grassy meadows where Eastenders fulfilled a dream of living in a house in the country.

•DISTANCE•	3¾ miles (6km)
•MINIMUM TIME•	1hr 30min
•ASCENT / GRADIENT•	230ft (70m) ▲▲▲
•LEVEL OF DIFFICULTY•	👥 👥 👥
•PATHS•	Forest, field and horse tracks
•LANDSCAPE•	Woodland, meadows, ponds, farmland and ruins of urban housing developments
•SUGGESTED MAP•	aqua3 OS Explorer 175 Southend-on-Sea & Basildon
•START / FINISH•	Grid reference: TQ 599873
•DOG FRIENDLINESS•	Great forest and field romp with plenty of other dogs; bowl of water outside Visitors' Centre
•PARKING•	Free parking at the Visitors' Centre at Dunton
•PUBLIC TOILETS•	Visitors' Centre at Dunton

BACKGROUND TO THE WALK

Langdon Nature Reserve is a wonderful example of how abandoned urbanisations can become a haven for wildlife. Much of the area, now managed by Essex Wildlife Trust, was formerly known as Plotlands. But where did this strange name come from? Back in the 1890s, a great agricultural depression ravaged the farming communities of Essex. The farmlands, around what is now the urban fringes of Basildon, were taken out of production and became redundant. They were divided into small plots and sold cheaply at auction to Eastenders from London who dreamed of a self-sufficient lifestyle in the country.

The Good Life
Between the turn of the century and 1940, these 'Plotlanders', as they became known, built hundreds of modest chalets and bungalows as weekend retreats or holiday homes. Many families would travel up from London by train carrying building materials with them. They lived in makeshift bell tents while the man of the house went about the DIY.

Permanent residency was forbidden at Langdon because there was no proper sanitation or other services. For many Plotlanders, it was a bucket in the back and an old gas lamp to light the way if they needed the loo. But rural Essex was still a relatively quiet backwater, and most residents seemed happy to forego some modern conveniences in return for an escape from the bustle and overcrowding of the East End. At the outbreak of World War Two the authorities turned a blind eye as many Eastenders moved to Langdon to escape the horror of the Blitz and survived by growing their own fruit and vegetables. But in 1949 the Plotlands at Langdon were compulsorily purchased and demolished to make way for Basildon New Town. In this walk you can see what's left of these idealistic dwellings, with their overgrown gardens and orchards which, nearly half a century later, support a rich mixture of wild flowers and animals.

With 460 acres (186ha) of meadows, woods, ponds, plantation and scrub, Langdon is Essex Wildlife Trust's largest inland reserve. What makes Langdon so unusual, is not so much the rarity of its plant and animal life, but the many species – once commonplace in the countryside and now threatened by intensive farming and development – which thrive here. You may be lucky enough to spot badgers, foxes and weasels not to mention hundreds of orchids, butterflies and flowering plants. In the former Plotland ruins and gardens you'll even find adders and lizards.

Ancient Woodlands

In 1969, when plans were discovered that the meadows were to be turned into a housing development, there was public outcry and the idea was thankfully shelved. Today, the large grassy areas of Willow Park are still traditionally managed by grazing and haycutting and, in summer, wild flowers attract butterflies and insects. In spring the ancient woodlands of Marks Hill, Lincewood and Longwood are carpeted with primroses, wood anemones and bluebells, helped along by rotational coppicing, another form of ancient woodland management, which enables plants and animals to thrive. In your tramp through these ancient woodlands you'll not only discover ponds filled with great crested frogs and toads, but, as Langdon Hills is the highest point in Essex, you'll be privy to some of the most far-reaching panoramas of London.

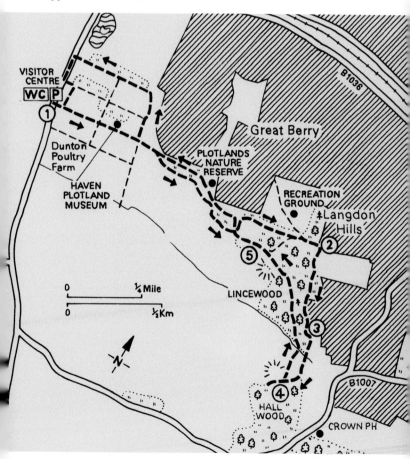

Walk 21

Walk 21 Directions

① From the car park, walk up the straight wide avenue of **Plotlands**, passing the museum on your left. After 500 yards (457m) go straight ahead at red **waymark No 1**. You are now on the wide tarmac bridle path, with fields on your right, and occasional views of south Essex between the trees. Ignoring other paths continue along this bridle path, passing **Val's Gate** on your right, then look left for the recreation ground, which is full of orchids in spring. Continue along the path for 100yds (91m) until you reach wide cross paths.

② Turn right at red **waymark No 2**. You are now in **Lincewood**. The path undulates through high trees and open woodland, passing behind houses on your left, with glimpses of the pond on your right at red **waymark No 3**.

③ At **waymark No 4** there are four steep wooden steps. Ignore these and turn right along the path, keeping the wooden fencing enclosing **Hall Wood** on your left. Walk for 20yds (18m), to a break in the trees, for views of the London skyline. Retrace your steps and take the first path on your left downhill, towards the wooden kissing gate.

④ Follow this narrow track downhill through ferns, and after 200yds (183m) reach the duckboard

skirting the pond. Note the large oak tree growing from the banks of the pond forming a low arch across the duckboard. Continue ahead through the kissing gate and walk downhill as the path meanders and undulates through open woodland, with ferns and patches of meadow awash with bluebells in spring. Continue along this path to the wooden bench beneath the large oak tree, where there are superb views of rolling farmland and London in the distance.

WHILE YOU'RE THERE ⓘ

Visit the **Haven Museum** and see what a pre-war Plotland dwelling looked like. This simple cottage offers a fascinating insight into the lives of Plotlanders. The lounge, furnished with books and knick-knacks, feels as though the family have just popped out to do the shopping.

---

⑤ At the Y-junction, take the left-hand path downhill keeping the arable field on your left. Go through the pair of timber posts and turn left on to the wide grassy bridleway. At the kissing gate, turn right and after 10yds (9m) turn left on to another grassy path. Maintain direction through two meadows, keeping the houses on your right. At the end of the second meadow is red **waymark No 1**. Here, turn right keeping the Plotland ruins on your left. Pass the Plotland Trail **waymarks 5** and **6**, turn left at the next bridle path and follow the waymarks back to the car park.

WHAT TO LOOK FOR ⓘ

Wander into **Hall Wood** where you can see a rare woodland of oak and native cherry and views of East London with Canary Wharf Tower in the distance. In May and June the woods are a riot of colour with orchids and bluebells.

WHERE TO EAT AND DRINK ⓘ

The impressive weather-boarded **Crown** pub, a Harvester franchise in the High Road, offers 'lunch for less than a fiver' and 'early bird specials'. You can also buy drinks and snacks from the **Visitors' Centre** at Dunton or bring your own and have an alfresco lunch in the picnic area.

Wandering in Weald Country Park

A fairly strenuous walk taking in the history of a great Tudor mansion and a royal deer park.

•DISTANCE•	5 miles (8km)
•MINIMUM TIME•	2hrs 45min
•ASCENT / GRADIENT•	117ft (35m) ▲▲▲
•LEVEL OF DIFFICULTY•	🚶🚶 🚶🚶 🚶
•PATHS•	Open parkland, forest tracks and some cross-field footpaths
•LANDSCAPE•	Undulating deer parkland, ponds, lakes and mixed woodland
•SUGGESTED MAP•	aqua3 OS Explorer 175 Southend-on-Sea & Basildon
•START / FINISH•	Grid reference: TQ 568940
•DOG FRIENDLINESS•	Wonderful open spaces for a romp but watch out for grazing cattle and ducks
•PARKING•	Free car parks at Visitor Centre, Belvedere and Cricket Green on Weald Road and Lincolns Lane
•PUBLIC TOILETS•	Visitor Centre and inside park

BACKGROUND TO THE WALK

Weald Country Park's origins are back in 1062 when the land was a gift from King Harold to the Abbots of Waltham. The abbots managed the land (which was worked by peasants), added fallow deer which they hunted for food and sport, and over the years the estate prospered. All this came to an end when Henry VIII dissolved the monasteries and stripped them of their lands and goods. Weald was passed to the King's closest allies.

Discover a Country Park

In this walk you will discover a mixture of formal landscapes, with lakes and woodlands, and spot fallow deer – elements which make this country park one of the finest in Essex. You will also take a trip into history as you explore the site of Weald Hall, a fine Tudor mansion, built in 1540 and extended over the years by various owners. In Tudor times owning a deer park brought more prestige than having your own moat, but less than having your own private gallows.

A Multitude of Owners

By 1800 the mansion had 40 bedrooms and provided jobs and housing for around 50 people. The first owner was Sir Brian Tuke, Henry VIII's treasurer, who was followed by a succession of *nouveau riche* individuals who made their money by trade or in government. One of these, Sir Anthony Browne, a judge, politician and favourite of Mary I, and who lived here in 1550, went on to become the founder of Brentwood School and provided almhouses for the poor. Although knighted by Queen Elizabeth, he persecuted Protestants during Mary's reign and was responsible for the death of a young apprentice, William Hunter, who was burned at the stake in Brentwood. A memorial to Hunter stands in the town.

But easily the most tyrannous of owners was William Scroggs, Lord Chief Justice to Charles II in 1678. He sent over 20 men to the gallows, and was so detested that when he died all traces of him were removed, including his face from a portrait at the top of the stairs in Weald Hall.

In 1756, the Towers, a family of lawyers, bought the estate and owned it for the next 200 years. During World War Two over 30,000 troops were stationed at Weald. Sadly Weald Hall fell into disrepair and the deer escaped, but in 1987 they were replaced. The house was demolished in the 1950s, but you can go to the top of Belvedere Hill where there are wonderful views over the parkland and you can get a real sense of the extent and grandeur of this royal hunting estate hundreds of years ago.

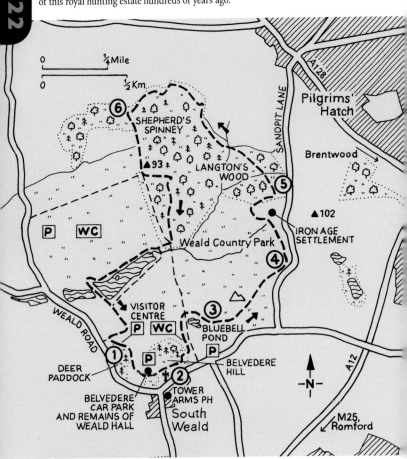

Walk 22 **Directions**

① With your back to **Weald Road**, turn right out of the car park past the golden willow tree. Keep the red brick wall on your right and continue to the **Belvedere car park**

– the site of the foundations of Weald Hall. On your left an information board tells the story of the Hall and refers to tunnels linking it with St Thomas Becket's Church in Brentwood. Walk into the car park and take the earth path uphill. Turn left, keeping the church

Walk 22

WHERE TO EAT AND DRINK ℹ

None on route, but if you pack a picnic you can enjoy it at the pleasant tables outside the **Visitor Centre**, which also serves drinks and light refreshments. Pub options include the **Tower Arms** in Weald Road and the **Nag's Head** opposite Wigley Bush Lane. Otherwise head for the **Little Chef** on the A1023 just before junction 28 of the M25.

WHAT TO LOOK FOR ℹ

Pick up a **tree trail** from the Visitor Centre and have fun identifying a multitude of trees. The park has 500-year-old hornbeam, weeping willow, dawn redwood, sweet chestnut, horse chestnut and silver birch to name but a few species. Superstition and folklore surround many trees such as the alder which, when cut, was supposed to represent the blood of the devil while others, such as ash, was believed to drive evil spirits away when burned.

on your right, and pass the door which used to give access to the graves of the Tower family. At the end of the church wall, turn left through trees and go on to the grassy knoll. This overlooks the original gardens of the estate and the site of Weald Hall.

② Keeping the gardens to your left, walk up the steps to the site of **Belvedere Hill** where spectators would watch hunting and indulge in banquets. Walk down the steps, turn right and take the path downhill, between conifers, to open parkland. Maintain direction and turn left through the gap in the fence keeping **Bluebell Pond** and the cricket field on your right.

③ Turn right through the kissing gate and follow the grassy path uphill, passing the bridleway waymarks on your right. At the top of the hill, pass through a thickly

wooded area of ancient hornbeam and silver birch, and continue along the bridleway, which runs parallel with **Sandpit Lane**.

④ As the path veers away from the road, note the steep embankment to your right – the remains of an Iron Age settlement. You are now walking around what was the moat. Keep to the path through meadow and parkland and, at the tree-clad embankment rising to your right, continue clockwise until you join the hard track.

⑤ Turn left through the gap in the fence on your left and continue walking downhill through **Langton's Wood**. Follow this hard bridleway, which hugs the edge of the woods, until you pass an avenue of sweet chestnut trees by **Shepherd's Spinney**.

⑥ At the fingerpost turn left on to the public footpath. After 400yds (366m), at the cross path, turn left and then right between the wide avenue of chestnut trees. After 500yds (457m), turn right before the kissing gate to walk with the lake on your left. At the end of the lake, turn left over the footbridge and return to the car park passing the deer paddock.

WHILE YOU'RE THERE ℹ

Adults and children alike may enjoy a visit to **Old Macdonalds Park Farm** where attractions include the TV star of *Big Breakfast*, Connie the Dairy Shorthorn and friends; along with rare breeds of poultry, pigs, sheep and goats, a magnificent collection of owls, some of which are hand tame, and otters. You can also see the endangered red squirrel, which is part of a captive breeding programme on the farm.

Tilbury Riverside

A riverside walk from the home of the Bata Shoe Company, where boots were made for walking, to Tilbury Fort.

•DISTANCE•	8½ miles (13.7km)
•MINIMUM TIME•	3hrs
•ASCENT / GRADIENT•	34ft (10m)
•LEVEL OF DIFFICULTY•	𝍠𝍠 𝍠𝍠 𝍠𝍠
•PATHS•	Riverside path, field paths, sections of road, 1 stile
•LANDSCAPE•	River, estuary, marshland, industrial installations, residential area and historic forts
•SUGGESTED MAP•	aqua3 OS Explorer 163 Gravesend & Rochester
•START / FINISH•	Grid reference: TQ 689768
•DOG FRIENDLINESS•	Check times of high tide beforehand, some difficulty on jetty beside power station
•PARKING•	Free parking at Coalhouse Fort
•PUBLIC TOILETS•	Visitors' Centre, Coalhouse Fort

BACKGROUND TO THE WALK

East Tilbury seems like the end of the world but this village, on the Essex shore of the River Thames, is best known for being the home of the British Bata Shoe Company, and is a fine example of a complete planned urbanisation centred upon an industrial concern. In 1933 the first Bata building was opened by Czech entrepreneur, Tomas Bata, who also built a housing estate and provided funds for the construction of East Tilbury Station. His enterprise developed into a 'garden village' which included over 300 houses, a hotel, shops, swimming pool, memorial garden, orchard, sports facilities, a college, fire station and its own 300 acre (121ha) farm.

He may never have intended that the houses should look like shoeboxes, but they certainly do. You'll see these uniform cube-shaped, beige and cream pebble-dash dwellings with flat roofs in Coronation Road, King George VI Avenue and Thomas Bata Avenue, and there's no escaping the fact that they demonstrate a distinct eastern European influence. Nowadays, the factory manufactures industrial wellington boots with steel toe-caps.

Two Forts Guarding London

On days off, workers would scramble around Coalhouse Fort (1874), probably the best armoured casemate fortress in the south east, or stroll along the river to Tilbury Fort, a fine example of 17th century military engineering, with its star-shaped bastion fortress. Today you can trace Tilbury's defences, enjoy river views across to Kent, see World War Two gun emplacements and even fire a real anti-aircraft gun.

You'll get the best views of Tilbury Fort from the sea wall near Tilbury Power Station. Here ships bring coal from all over the world, to fuel the generators. The fort, now an English Heritage attraction, housed Scottish soldiers rounded up after the Battle of Culloden in 1746, many of whom died within its walls or on prison ships bound for the West Indies. It was also the scene of a bloody battle in the 18th century between Essex and Kent cricketers, during which an Essex man died and the fort commander was shot dead.

Along the river you can spot prolific bird life, amazing when you realise that you are only a few miles from the M25. You'll also discover that the area has had more than its fair share of environmental abuse with gravel extraction, refuse disposal, uncontrolled motorcycling and rough shooting, all leaving their mark. Leaving Tilbury Fort, you'll see herds of horses, abandoned over the years. On balmy summer evenings foals frolic across the marshes adding a touch of rural surrealism on an otherwise stark industrial landscape.

Walk 23 Directions

① From the **Visitors' Centre**, turn left keeping the moat on your left. Bear right and walk along the

sleepers of the disused railway track to the grassy embankment with the river on your left. Follow the footpath above the shingle of the river, towards what appears to be a water tower, but is in fact a radar

WHAT TO LOOK FOR ℹ

In the common lands around Tilbury Fort look for grey heron, swan and pied wagtail. Other species include tern, which feed near the power station outflow. Look for flocks of black-headed gulls and starlings at the sewage works, and cormorants, which sit on the railings by the station jetty. You may also spot curlew and plover.

tower of World War Two vintage. Near by you can see the remains of the jetty used when transporting ammunition from Purfleet and also the site of the 1540 blockhouse.

② After 1 mile (1.6km) with East Tilbury marshes on your right, a favourite place for migrant wading birds, cross the metal gate beyond which are the remains of World War Two concrete jetties surrounded by grassy banks, popular with fishermen. The path is mainly concrete and the power station looms large. On both sides of the path, earth has been dug up, seemingly by giant moles. The giant moles are, in fact, treasure hunters foraging for discarded bottles, ceramics and other paraphernalia, some of it dating back to the 1930s. Flotsam on the foreshore provides beachcombers with similar opportunities. Continue along the concrete path following the high sea wall fronting the power station and **Bill McRoy Creek**, where the

WHILE YOU'RE THERE ℹ

No time to tour the inside of Tilbury Fort? Then pop into the main entrance, known as the Water Gate, recognisable by its central archway and narrower flanks framed by columns. Reminiscent of a Roman triumphal arch, and built in fine Portland stone, you can at least peer into the inner courtyard and get an idea of the defences.

Thames flooded much of the area to the north in 1953, until you reach metal steps leading to the car park at **Tilbury Fort**.

③ Turn right into **Fort Road** and after 1 mile (1.6km) you can see houses at the southern end of West Tilbury village. Looking ahead, to the right, is the church, originally built by the Normans, strategically placed on the escarpment for views across the estuary. Turn right into **Cooper Shaw Road**. To the right, across Tilbury Marshes, the twin chimneys of the power station dominate the landscape.

WHERE TO EAT AND DRINK ℹ

The World's End pub makes a fine watering hole and is conveniently located beside Tilbury Fort. Some parts date to the 15th century and are reputedly haunted. The famished should go for gut-busting steak and kidney pie washed down with a pint, before heading off across the marshes and back to Coalhouse Fort.

④ At the T-junction, turn left into **Church Road** and walk about 500yds (457m) into **West Tilbury** with its picturesque green overlooked by the **Kings Head** pub. Walk past the pub and about 100yds (91m) on the right, take the cross-field footpath until you reach **Low Street Lane** where you turn left. Walk along Low Street Lane for 300yds (274m) and take the footpath on the right. Walk towards the houses of **East Tilbury** on the cross-field path and emerge at **Beechcroft Avenue**. Cross this road into **Stenning Way** and, after about 200yds (183m), take the path on the right to **Princess Margaret Road.** Turn right, passing East Tilbury railway station, and return to the car park at **Coalhouse Fort**.

Coalhouse Fort

A short loop extends the walk to Coalhouse Fort and St Catherine's Church.
See map and information panel for Walk 23

•DISTANCE•	9½ miles (15.3km)
•MINIMUM TIME•	3hrs 30min
•ASCENT / GRADIENT•	34ft (10m)
•LEVEL OF DIFFICULTY•	

Walk 24 **Directions** (Walk 23 option)

Coalhouse Fort at East Tilbury was completed in 1874, on the site of previous earthen batteries. It is one of 76 coastal forts and batteries built at a time when Britain feared invasion from continental Europe. Many of these defences have been demolished but this is one of the last remaining examples of an armoured casemate fort. It has the distinction of never firing a shot, although it became a military establishment during both World War One and World War Two.

From the embankment, Point Ⓐ, keep the river on your right and walk along the sea wall. Below you on the left, after 200yds (183m), are the Quickfire Battery and Search Light Station dating back to 1893. Parts of the battery have been overbuilt for two flat-topped Defence Electric Light emplacements. If you're feeling adventurous take the footpath, which leads to these structures, to see the mountings for the guns.

Follow the grassy footpath back on the embankment and, at the T-junction, bear right to follow the path on the outer perimeter of the moat. Keep to this path and you will notice, on your left, the concrete triangular structure across the moat, which was an additional sea defence. As you walk around the moat you can see how well hidden the fort would be to enemy shipping coming up river.

At the end of the footpath, Point Ⓑ, look left across the end of the moat, where there are two concrete structures which were part of the Minefield Control System, used during World War Two when mines were strung out between Essex and Kent to prevent invasion by sea. Continue ahead up steps to the concrete sea wall defence. Looking right it stretches for some way enclosing a grassy and marshy area popular with twitchers. Turn left at the sea wall and, after 20yds (18m), go up concrete steps to the grassy embankment to 12th-century **St Catherine's Church**, Point Ⓒ, with a stump of a tower. During World War One the local vicar asked the troops stationed at Coalhouse Fort to build a tower, but half-way through they were forced to stop because permission from their commanding officer had not been obtained. At the gates, turn left to return to the car park or right for the **Ship**, East Tilbury's only pub.

Walk 25

Dipping into Davy Down

Combine wonderful woodland walking and riverside views with a visit to one of the south east's busiest shopping centres.

•DISTANCE•	4 miles (6.4km)
•MINIMUM TIME•	2hrs
•ASCENT / GRADIENT•	50ft (15m) ▲ ▲ ▲
•LEVEL OF DIFFICULTY•	🚶 🚶 🚶
•PATHS•	Forest tracks, river bank and grassy paths prone to muddiness, boardwalk
•LANDSCAPE•	Meadow, woodland, flood plains and river
•SUGGESTED MAP•	aqua3 OS Explorer 162 Greenwich & Gravesend
•START / FINISH•	Grid reference: TQ 594798
•DOG FRIENDLINESS•	Good place for a romp off lead in woods
•PARKING•	Free car parks at Davy Down Visitors' Centre and Stifford Bridge
•PUBLIC TOILETS•	Davy Down Visitors' Centre

Walk 25 Directions

Davy Down is part of the Thames Chase Community Forest, one of 12 such forests in England covering large areas close to towns and cities. Far from being continuous plantings of trees in the traditional sense, community forests are a conglomeration of wooded landscapes which may include farmland, villages, nature areas and public open spaces. The aim of the community forest is to create easily accessible landscapes for wildlife, work, education and recreation.

Davy Down nestles in the Mardyke Valley, among large modern developments to the north east of Lakeside Shopping Centre. Once used for market gardening, the land was taken over in 1985 as part of the Thames Chase Community Forest when the busy A13 trunk road was built, thus bringing to an end a long history of farming which

dates back to 1730. The derelict outbuildings were replaced by the Davy Down visitors' car park. From this abandoned farmland, new landscapes are being created – you will see ponds and wetlands, new woodland hedgerows and areas planted with over 4,000 trees.

Start from the visitors' car park, where you can still see remnants of the old farm in the form of gate posts and garden plants. Go through the gate and follow the path as it winds its way through the site, passing the **Stifford Pumping Station** which still extracts water from the 150ft (46m) bore hole in the chalk below. After climbing earth steps towards the pumping

---

WHILE YOU'RE THERE ⓘ

Lakeside Shopping Centre is west of Davy Down. This centre attracts millions of shoppers each year and contains more than 300 shops, a food court, a multiplex cinema and a watersports' complex at the centre of the lake.

WHERE TO EAT AND DRINK ℹ️
There are no places to stop for refreshments on this walk but, if you're driving, try the **Dog and Partridge** pub at Stifford (no food 3PM–6PM, Monday–Friday), or the **Royal Oak** (food served all day) at South Ockendon overlooking The Green. Both are dog- and child-friendly establishments. Otherwise, head for **Lakeside** where there are dozens of eateries to choose from.

station, walk to the left towards trees and on to the boardwalk which bisects three ponds.

In the distance the 1892 railway viaduct spans the valley. Below is a small modern footbridge which you cross to link up with the **Mardyke Way**. The River Mardyke winds its way through the Plain of Thurrock, from its source, 8 miles (12.9km) upstream, to the River Thames at Purfleet, meandering through Davy Down where the valley is dominated by flood plain meadows bounded by ancient woodlands.

Until the 15th century the valley was mainly wet fenland, much like the rest of Essex. The land was drained for agriculture and the course of the river was straightened. Work has begun to increase access in the valley and to improve the landscape and wildlife habitat. This will include efforts to return the channelled river to a more natural feature, by creating shelves and bays and planting trees and hedgerows.

Cross the footbridge, turn left and after the 'Welcome to Mardyke Meadows' sign, take the first path right into **Brannets Wood**, one of the oldest recorded ancient woodlands in south Essex. The track, through thick foliage and tall trees, rises sharply and soon bears

left in a westerly direction. After ½ mile (800m), a cross path indicates the start of the less dense **Millards Green** ahead. Turn left here and, after 30yds (27m), rejoin the grassy **Mardyke Way** cross path keeping the fence on your right.

Beyond the fence the meadow flood plain stretches to the **Mardyke River** which, in summer, is accessible on foot, but soon floods after heavy rains. Retrace your steps beneath the viaduct along the wide grassy river. Ignore the modern footbridge, and continue to the next bridge, **Stifford Bridge**, where medieval pilgrims once crossed on their way to Canterbury. Cross the bridge and go left on to the wide boardwalk to the car park, where there is an interpretative sign. Turn right and follow the grassy track, keeping the fencing on your right, to return to **Stifford Bridge**. Do not recross the bridge, but instead turn left and walk towards the viaduct in the distance.

Just before the viaduct the path bears left and, after 200yds (183m), take the grassy path right, uphill, and walk between rows of oak saplings, part of a new woodland scheme. The path continues uphill and passes quite close to the Stifford road. Looking left, there is a marvellous view of Davy Down and the pumping station. Follow the path back to the car park.

WHAT TO LOOK FOR ℹ️
Water voles love wet areas such as rivers, ditches and ponds and there's no shortage of these at Davy Down. Loss of suitable habitat through urban development, increased river bank mowing, dredging and degradation of river banks spell danger for these small creatures – now a protected species.

Willingale – a Pint-sized Parish with Two Churches

An easy stroll along the Essex Way which includes one of the county's most rural villages.

•DISTANCE•	3¾ miles (6km)
•MINIMUM TIME•	1hr 30min
•ASCENT / GRADIENT•	33ft (11m) ▲ ▲ ▲
•LEVEL OF DIFFICULTY•	🚶 🚶 🚶
•PATHS•	Field-edge paths, riverside meadows and green lane
•LANDSCAPE•	Rolling countryside, arable farmland and river
•SUGGESTED MAP•	aqua3 OS Explorer 183 Chelmsford & The Rodings, Maldon & Witham
•START / FINISH•	Grid reference: TL 597076
•DOG FRIENDLINESS•	Should be on lead for most of walk
•PARKING•	Free car park at Willingale Village Hall
•PUBLIC TOILETS•	None on route

BACKGROUND TO THE WALK

So tiny is the peaceful and picturesque village of Willingale in central Essex, that if you blink you'll miss it. Its cottages and houses are spread out over quite a large area, and the focal point of the village, its two churches – St Andrew's and St Christopher's – are unique in Essex as they share the same churchyard.

Sibling Rivalry

All sorts of myths abound as to how this came about, but a story, which has now become part of village folklore, tells of an argument between two sisters which resulted in each deciding to build her own church. It's a story that may keep the passing visitor entertained, but since St Christopher's was built 200 years after St Andrew's, one of the quarrelling sisters must have discovered the key to longevity. What they argued about nobody really knows, but maybe their differences were down to that age-old problem concerning women – men.

Additional Spiritual Care

Perhaps we shall never know the real cause of their rivalry, but a more likely explanation for the churches, is in the names of the two parishes, Willingale Spain and Willingale Doe. In the 12th century Hervey d'Espania built Spains Hall and the church in Willingale Spain and also gave his name to the parish. Then in the 14th century, at a time when the wool industry was expanding, the d'Ou family settled in Willingale. Workers were attracted to the area and St Andrew's simply couldn't cope with the population explosion. The d'Ou family built St Christopher's Church on the site of the already consecrated land and this is probably where the name Willingale Doe originates.

Until 1929 each church had its own parish priest and congregation. Today they come under one parish and the churchyard is separated by the Essex Way, a long distance path which stretches across Essex from Epping in the south west to Harwich in the north east.

The churches are well worth visiting, and if you stroll through the churchyard you are in for a treat with magnificent views across the Roding Valley.

An American Air Base

During World War Two, Willingale buzzed with the sound of aircraft from the 387th Bombardment Division of the United States Army Air Force (USAAF). Officers were based at nearby Willingale Airfield, now abandoned; St Andrew's Church provided prayer and hope while the Bell public house, across the road, provided many a pint. With just over 500 people in the village and two pubs in which to socialise, Willingale was and still is, a pint-sized parish. But these days the village is distinctly 'dry' as the Bell and the Maltsers Arms are now private residences.

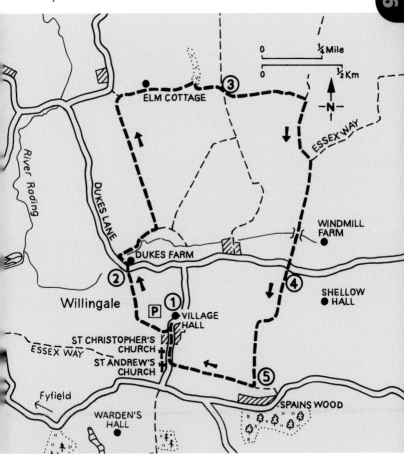

Walk 26 Directions

① Turn right outside the **village hall**. Follow the road around to the left and turn right at the footpath sign by the former village school, now a private residence. At the end of the gardens, turn right along the grassy path on to the field-edge path and continue to bear right for 500yds (457m) to **Dukes Lane**. To your left are panoramic views of the Roding Valley.

Walk 26

② Turn left into **Dukes Lane** and walk for 200yds (183m). Then, after passing **Dukes Farm** outbuildings, turn right at the fingerpost. Walk up the embankment and maintain direction along the field-edge path with the stream on your right for about 400yds (366m). Turn left on to the uphill cross-field path through a gap in the hedge and go across another field to cross a wooden footbridge. Maintain direction along two field-edge paths until you reach the junction with **Elms Farm Road** on your left and **Elm Cottage** on your right.

> **WHILE YOU'RE THERE** ⓘ
>
> **St Andrew's Church**, built of flint rubble with Roman tiles and reused bricks, dates from the 12th century but is no longer used for worship. Inside you can see some early 17th-century engraved brass memorial inscription plates, set in stone slabs on the chancel floor. Look for the Norman windows on the north and south walls and the ornate ironwork on the north door.

③ Turn right on to the bridleway, pass Elm Cottage and, at the T-junction where the bridleway bears left, turn right on to the path. Continue for 200yds (183m) then follow the field-edge path for 300yds (274m) until you meet the **Essex Way**. Follow this wide byway south, passing **Windmill Farm** on your left and pass over the footbridge towards **Shellow Road**.

> **WHERE TO EAT AND DRINK** ⓘ
>
> There is nothing in Willingale itself, Fyfield is the nearest place for food and drink. Try the **Queens Head** for good pub lunches and snacks, the **Black Bull** for home-cooked dishes and real ale or the **Haque Empire** for slap up Indian cuisine. Otherwise, shop at Fyfield's post office or bring a packed lunch.

> **WHAT TO LOOK FOR** ⓘ
>
> Willingale has some lovely old houses, some of which can be seen on or near this walk. The **Pound House** dates back to the 17th century; **Duke's Farmhouse**, a 16th-century restored timber-framed house, has a good example of a jettied front (the upper storey projects beyond the storey below); while **Warden's Hall**, to the south of the village, is a 16th-century red brick house hiding behind an 18th-century façade.

④ Cross **Shellow Road** and continue along the **Essex Way**, with views of Shellow Hall to your left. After 300yds (274m), bear right and then left, keeping the hedgerow to your right. After another 100yds (91m), turn right through the gap in the hedge, then continue with the hedgerow on your left.

⑤ In front of the cottages at **Spains Wood**, cross the footbridge over the ditch and turn right, continuing along the **Essex Way**. After another bridge, maintain direction keeping the hedgerow on your left. Follow the path through the cricket field and into **Willingale** where the **Essex Way** continues past the **Bell** on your right (now a private house) and crosses the churchyard between St Christopher's and St Andrew's churches. After exploring the churches and churchyard retrace your steps to **The Street**, which becomes **Beech Road** and return to the village hall car park.

A Castle at Pleshey

A gentle walk combining rolling countryside and one of the finest motte and bailey castles in Britain.

•DISTANCE•	3 miles (4.8km)
•MINIMUM TIME•	1hr 30min
•ASCENT / GRADIENT•	56ft (17m) ▲▲ ▲ ▲
•LEVEL OF DIFFICULTY•	🚶 🚶 🚶
•PATHS•	Grassy tracks, field and woodland paths prone to muddiness, some roads, 1 stile
•LANDSCAPE•	Gently rolling farmland, woodland and brook
•SUGGESTED MAP•	aqua3 OS Explorer 183 Chelmsford & The Rodings, Maldon & Witham
•START / FINISH•	Grid reference: TL 662142
•DOG FRIENDLINESS•	Stacks of mud and lots of water to cool paws, but should be on lead along fields
•PARKING•	Free car park at the village hall
•PUBLIC TOILETS•	None on route

BACKGROUND TO THE WALK

Long before the Norman conquest in 1066, Pleshey was occupied by a Saxon settlement, but the village is better known for its motte and bailey castle. William the Conqueror gave the land to Geoffrey de Mandeville whose castle once crowned the towering, flat-topped grassy mound, or motte, dominating the village and countryside. Constructed from soil dug out to make a deep ditch, or moat, the motte was enclosed by earth and timber stockades inside which was a wooden tower, later replaced by one of stone. Here lived the Mandevilles, while the open area in front of it, the bailey, or courtyard, was crammed with stables, barns and storehouses. Today nothing remains of the castle apart from the 14th-century brick bridge, believed to be the oldest in Britain.

The Tragic Fate of a Nobleman

Intrigue and heartbreak plagued Pleshey Castle. In 1142, Geoffrey de Mandeville's grandson, also named Geoffrey, was arrested for his allegiance to King Stephen's rival, Matilda. He secured his release by forfeiting both Pleshey and Saffron castles and the Tower of London, only to be killed two years later. Eventually Pleshey passed to the Duke of Gloucester, who met his fate at Calais in 1397, murdered on the orders of his nephew, Richard II, who seized the castle and all his possessions. The Duchess of Gloucester was so grief-stricken that she fled to a nunnery at Barking, but returned to Pleshey to die.

Pleshey, which over the centuries developed to the north of the motte and bailey, is surrounded by a stream and a partly water-filled ditch known as the Town Enclosure. Today the village, with its two pubs, picturesque 16th- and 17th-century cottages and village hall, evokes a real sense of community. But like many places throughout the country, Pleshey's castle, church and College of Canons were seized by Henry VIII and given to a greedy kinsman, John Gates. Gates destroyed everything, and only the earthworks and a few arches in the church remind us of Pleshey's former glory.

Peace and Public Houses

The walk takes in part of the Essex Way, a national recreational footpath, which slices through the village along The Street passing the White Horse pub and the Leather Bottle and follows Walthambury Brook. Before, or after the walk, take time to visit the interior of Holy Trinity Church where a stone on the wall, reputed to have come from Pleshey Castle, reads 'Ricardus Rex II', a reminder of its royal patronage. Next door is the country's first House of Retreat, owned by the Diocese of Chelmsford. A former convent, it played an important role as a convalescent home for Belgian soldiers injured in World War One, and today is a haven of peace and prayer welcoming all denominations.

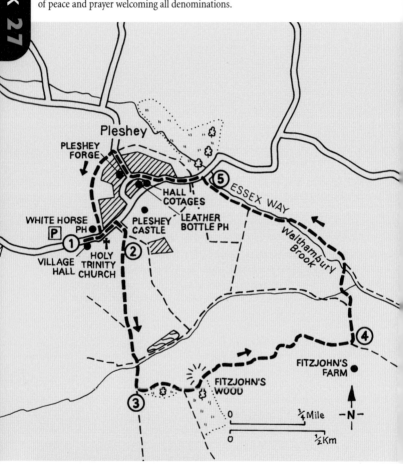

Walk 27 Directions

① From the car park at the village hall, walk to **The Street** and turn right passing **Holy Trinity Church** on your right and the **White Horse** pub on your left. After the church you will see the 16th-century

gatehouse, behind which is the convent, collectively they are known as the House of Retreat. Just after the restored water pump turn right into **Pump Lane**. After 100yds (91m), on your left you will see the bridge over the moat – the entrance into the earthworks of the motte and bailey castle.

② With your back to the castle, and keeping the church to your right, walk across the cricket field to the waymark beside the wooden gate. Turn right along the concrete path keeping the field on your left. Maintain direction, ignoring two footpaths on the right and one on the left by the reservoir.

③ At the second fingerpost, left, follow the bridleway bounded by trees. This path, which may be very muddy after rain, passes by **Fitzjohn's Wood** affording good views of rolling countryside. Beyond the outline of Holy Trinity Church you can appreciate the advantage of the hillside location of Pleshey Castle.

④ When you are level with the old house on the right, which was **Fitzjohn's Farm**, walk a few paces to the line of trees on your left and turn left on to the field-edge path, downhill. At the bottom of the hill, ignore the wooden footbridge over the brook to your left and follow the path which bears left over an earth bridge. After 100yds (91m) turn right over another earth bridge at **Walthambury Brook** and climb over the stile fence and up the embankment, so that the brook is now on your left. You are now on the grassy path of the **Essex Way**, which follows Walthambury Brook all the way to The Street at **Pleshey**.

> **WHILE YOU'RE THERE** ⓘ
> **Pleshey Castle** is private property but can be visited by prior appointment by telephoning 01245 360239. If you stand at the top of the motte you can see the Town Enclosure laid out below you to the west, north and east. Alternatively, look at the aerial photographs of the castle which are displayed inside the White Horse pub.

⑤ Turn left at The Street and turn right into **Back Lane**, passing Pleshey **Hall Cottages** on your left. At the fingerpost marked **Pleshey Grange**, turn right into **Vicarage Lane**, passing Pleshey Forge on your left. At the next fingerpost, turn left on to the grassy path which follows the Town Enclosure, with the ditch on your left. Cross the footbridge and maintain direction until you reach the **White Horse** pub on your left and emerge into **The Street**. Turn right to return to the car park.

> **WHAT TO LOOK FOR** ⓘ
> Look for the tombstone of Humphrey Sargant in the graveyard of **Holy Trinity Church**. He was a local trader who issued the Pleshey Farthing as a supplement to the State coinage during the mid-17th century. The coin has a crest on one side and a shield of arms on the other. They have been found in freshly ploughed fields.

> **WHERE TO EAT AND DRINK** ⓘ
> The **White Horse**, dating back to the 17th century, is full of character and atmosphere. It has an attractive beer garden and serves excellent home cooked food. You can even research your own recipe from the extensive collection of cookery books in the lounge. The **Leather Bottle**, another old pub, also serves first class meals.

Walk 28

The Longer Ongar walk

Rolling farmlands, big skies and a pretty Essex village where missionary David Livingstone lived and preached.

·DISTANCE·	6½ miles (10.4km)
·MINIMUM TIME·	3hrs 30min
·ASCENT / GRADIENT·	151ft (46m) ▲▲ ▲
·LEVEL OF DIFFICULTY·	👫 👫 👫
·PATHS·	Track and field paths prone to muddiness, stretches of road, 6 stiles
·LANDSCAPE·	Rolling farmland, patches of woodland, village streets
·SUGGESTED MAP·	aqua3 OS Explorer 183 Chelmsford & The Rodings, Maldon & Witham
·START / FINISH·	Grid reference: TL 552031
·DOG FRIENDLINESS·	Larger, or older, dogs (and their owners) will find stiles quite difficult
·PARKING·	Pay-and-display car parks at rear of Sainsbury's, police station and library in Chipping Ongar High Street
·PUBLIC TOILETS·	Public library at Chipping Ongar High Street

BACKGROUND TO THE WALK

Chipping Ongar's most famous resident was explorer and missionary David Livingstone (1813–73). Born in Blantyre in Scotland he came from a simple working class background and as a 10-year-old worked at a cotton mill, finishing at the end of the day to bury himself in books. In 1836 he studied medicine in Glasgow, working at his books during the winter and returning to the mill in the summer. At this time he attended a meeting by Dr Robert Moffat who ran a missionary station in Africa, and was inspired by his work there.

In 1838 Livingstone moved to Essex to extend his understanding of missionary work. He lived in a room near the United Reformed church in the High Street, Ongar and in his spare time would take long walks in the surrounding countryside. Livingstone stayed in Ongar for 15 months before leaving for London to complete his medical studies. In 1840 the London Missionary Sociey sent him to Africa where he spent his life immersed in his missionary work, establishing trade routes and writing books about the great continent, where he discovered Victoria Falls in 1855.

During his time in Ongar, Livingstone walked to London to visit a sick relative but got hopelessly lost at Stanford Rivers and had to climb a direction post to get his bearings. On another ocassion, when standing in for his minister at the Independent Chapel at Stanford Rivers, Livingstone apparently forgot his sermon, panicked and fled from the congregation. This was the shy nervous individual who went on to become a world famous explorer!

Churches and Farmland

Like Livingstone it's easy to get lost when exploring the muddy lanes around Ongar. On this walk you take the Essex Way, which is nicely waymarked, to Greensted and the oldest wooden church in the world. Livingstone would have walked around this delightful church discovering the Crusader coffin in the churchyard and the original timbers, which archaeologists confirm date back to 1066. Thereafter you traverse farmlands to Stanford Rivers climbing to a fine ridge of ancient oaks at Kettlebury Spring and views of rolling countryside. You finish your walk in the High Street with its timber-framed buildings and pass the room where Livingstone once lived.

That Famous Phrase

In 1871 a very sick Livingstone was found beside Lake Tanganyika by the American journalist Henry Morton Stanley who addressed him with the famous phrase, 'Dr Livingstone, I presume'. Stanley failed to convince Livingstone to return to England for treatment and the great explorer died in Africa two years later. Unlike Livingstone, no hack will be waiting to track you down but, as you emerge into the High Street after being ankle-deep in mud, the locals might just say, 'Essex walkers, I presume?'

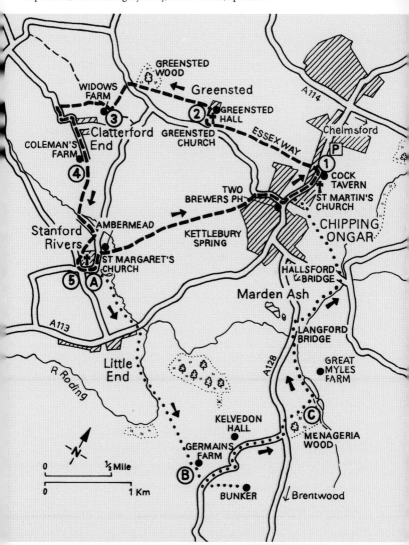

Walk 28

Walk 28 Directions

① From the rear of the car park take the **Essex Way** towards **Greensted**. As the path narrows, walk between dwarf oaks, over the cross path and through the kissing gate. Bear right, then left towards the second kissing gate, passing the pond of Greensted Hall on your right. Walk through the gate, passing Church Lodge on your left; **Greensted church** is on your right.

② Keeping the church on your right, bear right past terraced cottages and go through the gate. After 100yds (91m), turn left across the footbridge and follow the field-edge path keeping the hedgerow on your right. Maintain this direction through three fields, passing **Greensted Wood** on your right, until you reach **Greensted Road**. Turn left and pick up the footpath on your right. Continue along the field-edge path keeping hedgerows on your left for about 100yds (91m), where you cross the stile so that the hedgerow is now on your right. Climb a series of five stiles.

③ At the fifth stile turn right and after 100yds (91m), cross another stile. Turn right, passing the low wall of **Widow's Farm** on your left, and follow the path right. After 25yds (23m), take the footpath left and follow the field-edge path to **Toot Hill Road**. Turn left for

Clatterford End. At the T-junction maintain direction for **Coleman's Farm**, following the lane.

④ As the lane bears right into Coleman's Farm, maintain direction on to the bridleway for ½ mile (800m), ignoring paths left and right until you reach the tarmac lane. Just before the T-junction, turn right on to the cross-field path to **Stanford Rivers**. At the converted barn dwellings on your left, turn right on to the gravel path and left on to **School Road** with **St Margaret's Church** on your left.

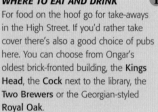

> ### WHERE TO EAT AND DRINK
> For food on the hoof go for take-aways in the High Street. If you'd rather take cover there's also a good choice of pubs here. You can choose from Ongar's oldest brick-fronted building, the **Kings Head**, the **Cock** next to the library, the **Two Brewers** or the Georgian-styled **Royal Oak**.

⑤ Walk past the church to the crossroads and turn left. After 400yds (366m) follow the right turn next to the house called **Ambermead**. Maintain direction on the uphill path for views of farmland and pass the ridge of oak trees at **Kettlebury Spring**. Follow the path past the school and turn right on to **The Borough**. Continue to the T-junction passing the Two Brewers pub on the right. Turn left into the **High Street** and return to the car park.

> ### WHAT TO LOOK FOR
> Behind Ongar's High Street seek out the 11th-century **St Martin's Church** with its narrow round headed windows, some of which are blocked up. This church is built of Roman bricks and rubble and its site, close to the castle, is an indication of Ongar's Norman importance.

> ### WHILE YOU'RE THERE
> Visit the site of the **Norman castle** just behind the High Street. Take the path beside the library and follow the signs to an impressive motte. The gateways and buildings have long disappeared, but an information board explains the layout of the castle.

Cold War Kelvedon Hatch

A longer walk taking in a secret cold war bunker.
See map and information panel for Walk 28

•DISTANCE•	9¾ miles (15.7km)
•MINIMUM TIME•	5hrs
•ASCENT / GRADIENT•	200ft (61m) ▲▲ ▲ ▲
•LEVEL OF DIFFICULTY•	🚶🚶 🚶 🚶

Walk 29 Directions (Walk 28 option)

After passing **St Margaret's Church** turn right at the yellow waymark. With the pond, Point Ⓐ, on your left take the field-edge path keeping the brook on your left for ½ mile (800m) to **Little End**. Cross the **A113** and the cattle grid. Cross the stile and the footbridge over the **River Roding** and follow the footpath for 1 mile (1.6km) to **Germaine's Farm**, Point Ⓑ, and bear left into **Kelvedon Hall Lane**.

Ignore the 'private' sign and walk up to the entrance of the Kelvedon Hatch bunker. Built in secret during the cold war, the three storeys were concealed 75 feet (23m) below ground. They were designed to house government and military personnel and a communications centre, in the event of nuclear war.

Retrace your steps to **Kelvedon Hall Lane** and turn right. Maintain direction along the road until you reach a T-junction, which emerges next to the grand **Kelvedon Hall Lodge** on the busy **A128**. Turn left, cross the road and turn right through the wide gap in the hedgerow. Walk ahead keeping

Menageria Wood, Point Ⓒ, on your right until you meet the cross path by three fishing lakes. From the red brick bridge ahead there are pleasant views of the lakes and Great Myles Farm with its distinctive clock tower.

Do not cross the bridge, but keeping the lake on your right, follow the path for ½ mile (800m) to meet the **A128** at **Langford Bridge**. Turn right and walk through a series of wooden gates over the bridge and, after 100 yards (91m) take the footpath right, keeping the river to your right until you reach **Hallsford Bridge**. Cross the road, go over the stile and take the cross-field path half left towards the church spire on the hill. Pass houses on your left then cross the stream via the concrete bridge. Bear left to the kissing gate, walk down past a row of cottages in **Bushey Lea** and rejoin Walk 28 in **Chipping Ongar High Street**.

> ### WHERE TO EAT AND DRINK ⓘ
> **Kelvedon Hatch bunker** certainly lives up to its cold war fame. In those days it operated round the clock to provide hot food for the bunker's personnel and nowadays it makes a great pit stop for hungry walkers. Mainly self-service, there's even an honesty box, but smile because you're on camera!

Walk 30

Bringing Home the Bacon at Little Dunmow

A rural walk and how married couples compete for a side of bacon.

•DISTANCE•	4 miles (6.4km)
•MINIMUM TIME•	1hr 45min
•ASCENT / GRADIENT•	89ft (27m) ▲ ▲ ▲
•LEVEL OF DIFFICULTY•	👣 👣 👣
•PATHS•	Grassy and farm tracks, field-edge paths liable to be muddy after rain
•LANDSCAPE•	Disused railway track, riverside meadow and farmland
•SUGGESTED MAP•	aqua3 OS Explorer 195 Braintree & Saffron Walden
•START / FINISH•	Grid reference: TL 655216
•DOG FRIENDLINESS•	A nice frolic on Flitch Way but watch out for cyclists and keep on lead by fields
•PARKING•	Informal street parking in Little Dunmow
•PUBLIC TOILETS•	None on route

Walk 30 Directions

The tiny village of Little Dunmow was the original home of an ancient ceremony known as the Dunmow Flitch Trial. A flitch, or side of bacon, was awarded to a married couple who could claim that they had lived in total peace and harmony for a year and a day. Nobody is sure how or why the ceremony came to be, but one theory is that the church authorities preferred couples to marry rather than live together as common law man and wife and a side of bacon, at a time when both food and money were scarce, provided an edible bonus. Winning such a prize in those days was equivalent to winning today's national lottery and one enterprising couple made a tidy profit by carving off slices to sell to hungry sightseers!

The ceremony fell out of favour by the mid-18th century but was revived in 1855, thanks to a publicity stunt by novelist Harrison Ainsworth (1805–82). His book, *The Flitch of Bacon* was a hit the year before, and in an effort to cash in on its success, he was instrumental in arranging for the Flitch Trial to be moved from Little Dunmow to Great Dunmow. Presiding as judge he awarded a flitch of bacon to an Ongar builder and his wife and, ever since, the Flitch Trial has been held at Great Dunmow every leap year.

> **WHAT TO LOOK FOR** ⓘ
> Inside **Little Dunmow's church** is the tomb of Walter Fitzwalter, a descendant of Robert Fitzwalter, lord of the manor, and some believe the founder of the Dunmow Flitch Trial. You can also see the oak chair in which successful claimants of the Flitch of Bacon were enthroned each year, and medieval Latin graffiti left by a monk which translates as 'a short life and a merry one.'

Walk 30

Park outside the **Flitch of Bacon** pub in **The Street**. From the pub turn right and right again into **Grange Lane** and after 100yds (91m), turn left at the fingerpost. Follow the yellow waymarks between houses and after 200yds (183m) turn right, pass the **Church of St Mary the Virgin** on your left, and join to the **Flitch Way**.

The church is all that remains of the old Augustinian priory of Little Dunmow and its main claim to fame is its association with the Flitch Trial. Founded in the 12th century it was, like other religious houses dissolved by Henry VIII in 1536. As you leave the church you pass **Priory Place**. This house was one of several which belonged to the priory, beyond it is the site of the priory fishponds. These were kept well stocked to provide food, but there is no record of a Flitch fish trial.

Turn right on to the **Flitch Way** a 15 mile (24km) linear nature park occupying the site of the old Bishop's Stortford-to-Braintree railway line. Today high hedgerows either side of the railway form a canopy full of wildlife. The line opened in 1869 and provided services for passengers, farmers and local industries who transported goods to main towns along the route. Passenger services stopped in 1952 and the line was eventually closed down in 1969.

Follow the Flitch Way for 1 mile (1.6km) until you reach the metal and brick bridge. Here take the steps down on the right and turn left under the bridge. Keep to the main footpath as it bears right towards the A120, with the **River Chelmer** on your left. Maintain direction until you pass two footbridges over the River Chelmer. Do not cross the bridges, but instead turn right on to the footpath, parallel with the river on your left.

Climb the wooden steps to rejoin the **Flitch Way**, turn left over the old railway bridge and descend 21 wooden steps to continue north along the footpath with the river on your left. As the river meanders towards the stone bridge, go straight ahead towards the yellow waymark. Follow the waymarks directly uphill until you reach the plantation of trees at the summit. Turn left, keeping the trees on your right, and maintain direction uphill on the often very muddy field-edge path for 500yds (457m).

Turn left on to the concrete track, **Grange Lane**, and follow it back to **Little Dunmow**. At the T-junction turn left into **The Street** where you will see an old water pump on the left just before the **Flitch of Bacon** pub. Continue to the pub for a well-earned rest.

Brawling and Benefactors Around Great Bardfield

An easy stroll combining gentle hills, a windmill called Gibraltar and the stronghold of a royal solicitor.

•DISTANCE•	4½ miles (7.2km)
•MINIMUM TIME•	2hrs
•ASCENT / GRADIENT•	100ft (30m) ▲ ▲ ▲
•LEVEL OF DIFFICULTY•	🚶 🚶 🚶
•PATHS•	Field-edge paths, river bank, grassy tracks and some town streets, 4 stiles
•LANDSCAPE•	Undulating grazing and arable farmland and river valley
•SUGGESTED MAP•	aqua3 OS Explorer 195 Braintree & Saffron Walden
•START / FINISH•	Grid reference: TL 677305
•DOG FRIENDLINESS•	A lot of places, including sheep fields, where dogs must be on leads
•PARKING•	Informal parking in Great Bardfield village
•PUBLIC TOILETS•	None on route

BACKGROUND TO THE WALK

Every so often you come across a delightful Essex village which begs to be explored. Great Bardfield is one such village, but there is nothing large about it. Quite the contrary, it is tiny but what it lacks in size is compensated by the sheer loveliness of the village itself and the surrounding countryside. The village is sited on a wide, gently sloping High Street with an attractive green overlooked by St Mary's Church, noted for its rare 14th-century stone rood screen, while a brick-built bridge across the River Pant links Great Bardfield with Finchingfield to the north.

A Generous Benefactor

Great Bardfield owes much of its heritage to William Bendlowes. He was born in the village in 1516 and went on to become Sergeant-at-Law to Mary Tudor and Queen Elizabeth I. He lived at Place House, one of the most historically important houses in the village, and died there in 1564. At Place House, it is said, Queen Elizabeth sought sanctuary from the persecution of her sister. Whether this is a story which got better with each telling is difficult to know, but what is indisputable is that Bendlowes left much of his wealth to the village.

Bendlowes was buried alongside his wife, Alienor, in St Mary's Church where his family later donated the chancel roof in 1618. He left a charitable trust and as you walk around the village you will see his legacy everywhere. There are cottage almhouses near the High Street; the Cottage Museum is another almshouse, inhabited until 1958, but now owned by the Bendlowes Trust and run by the local historical society. There's even a Bendlowes Road on a modern housing estate. Bendlowes and his wife would have admired the countryside hereabouts with its gentle hills, but would not have seen the windmill, incongruously named Gibraltar. Built in 1660, it last saw service as a mill in the 1930s, and is now a private residence overlooking pleasant Essex fields.

Farmworkers and farmers alike from Champions, Robjohns and Whinbush farms would have trudged along footpaths to get to church while the occupants of Bardfield Hall would have only needed to walk next door. These farms today have been modernised, while Bardfield Hall, now a picturesque private residence, still retains many of its 16th-century features.

Great Bardfield didn't feature on the itinerary of long haul carriages from Newmarket to London but that is not to say that the village was devoid of pubs. In the early 19th century when a brawl took place in one of the village's three inns and the miscreants needed a place to cool off, the village lock up in Bridge Street would have provided spartan accommodation for a handful of prisoners in its two tiny cells.

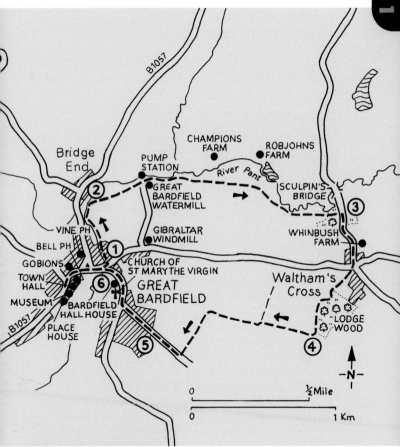

Walk 31 **Directions**

① From the village green take the fingerpost left off **Mill Road** and follow the path by the stream on your left with houses on your right. After 200yds (183m) at the field,

take the left fork still following the stream. Look over your right shoulder for a very good view of **Gibraltar Windmill**.

② Cross the stile through the hedge, turn right and continue with the hedge on your right until you reach the lane at **Great Bardfield Watermill**. Cross the lane and keep the mill pond and the **River Pant** on your left for 200yds (183m) to the pumping station. Turn right and then left around the perimeter, and take the cross-field path keeping the river and **Champions Farm** and **Robjohns Farm** on your left. Near the lake in front of Robjohns Farm, the path is indistinct, while the river meanders south and east. Stay on the grassy strip keeping the river on your left-hand side until you reach the stile at **Daw Street**, to the south of **Sculpins Bridge**.

WHERE TO EAT AND DRINK ℹ

The **Vine** public house in Great Bardfield has lots of character and dates back to the 16th century. It is a great place for traditional meals and specialities such as Spanish lamb, chicken cacciatore and trout. You could also try the **Bell**, next door to the Town Hall, for bar snacks and full meals in a friendly atmosphere.

---

③ Turn right, and after 400yds (366m) pass **Whinbush Farm**. When you reach the junction of the Bardfield–Waltham road, bear half right following a green fingerpost sign indicating '**Great Saling and Great Bardfield**'. Cross two stiles and maintain your direction along the path which skirts the edge of

---

WHILE YOU'RE THERE ℹ

Call in at Great Bardfield's local **museum** housed in a 16th-century cottage. It features an interesting display of 19th- and 20th-century domestic and agricultural implements along with local crafts. Don't miss The Cage which, as its name implies, was the local lock up for drunks and other miscreants.

WHAT TO LOOK FOR ℹ

See the fine timber-framed 12th-century barn in the middle of the **Bardfield Business Centre**, which used to be part of Bardfield Hall estate. The oldest house in the village is **Gobions**, next to the post office in the High Street, which dates back to the 15th century.

Lodge Wood. Keep the wood on your left and continue to its south western extremity where the path turns to the right.

④ Follow the path by the hedge under the row of poplar and larch trees and, as the outline of Great Bardfield and the windmill come into view, turn left. Follow the track with hedgerows on your left for about 300yds (274m) and turn right into the green lane.

⑤ Walk past the recreation ground on your right, cross the residential street and follow the footpath into **Braintree Road** where you turn right. On your left is the **Church of St Mary the Virgin** with its Norman tower and 14th-century nave. Local benefactors, the Bendlowes family, are buried inside the church.

⑥ Next to the church is the 16th-century manor house of **Bardfield Hall**, and for a further taste of Great Bardfield's history follow the road left through **Brook Street**, passing the starting point of the walk into the **High Street**. In quick succession you can see Gobions, one of the oldest houses in the village, Place House, the Cottage Museum and the Town Hall. After some refreshment retrace your steps to the green.

The Sound of Music at Thaxted

A glorious country walk following in the footsteps of composer Gustav Holst.

•DISTANCE•	3 miles (4.8km)
•MINIMUM TIME•	1hr 30min
•ASCENT / GRADIENT•	92ft (28m) ▲ ▲ ▲
•LEVEL OF DIFFICULTY•	🚶🚶 🚶🚶 🚶🚶
•PATHS•	Field-edge paths, bridleway prone to muddiness, river bank and some town streets
•LANDSCAPE•	Arable fields, meadows and undulating farmland
•SUGGESTED MAP•	aqua3 OS Explorer 195 Braintree & Saffron Walden
•START / FINISH•	Grid reference: TL 610311
•DOG FRIENDLINESS•	Great for romping, especially if you finish with a Thaxted sausage
•PARKING•	Free car park at Margaret Street
•PUBLIC TOILETS•	Car park in Margaret Street

BACKGROUND TO THE WALK

Thaxted must be one of Essex's prettiest villages, the sort you would expect to find gracing the top of a chocolate box, with its picturesque windmill, delightful thatched houses and a guildhall dating back to the 13th century. Perhaps this is what attracted composer and musician Gustav Holst (1874–1934) to the village. The young Gustav stayed overnight in Thaxted in 1913 during a five-day winter walking holiday in north west Essex, little knowing that a few years later he would come here to live.

An Inspiring View

Home for the composer, his wife and their daughter was, at first, a 17th-century thatched cottage. From here there were views across meadows and willow trees to the magnificent spire of St John the Baptist church in the village and this view, coupled with tranquillity and solitude, provided the inspiration for his work, *The Planets Suite* (1914–16).

Holst was born in Cheltenham to a father who came from the Baltic port of Riga. When he came to Thaxted he was known as Gustav von Holst, a name which at first aroused suspicion amongst the villagers who couldn't understand what motivated this stranger to walk alone, for so long and so far. On this walk you will enjoy panoramas of rolling countryside and big skies, and see the soaring spire of the church, visible for miles around, and perhaps experience similar feelings of liberation and solitude as the young Gustav whose genius was to make him one of our greatest composers.

Turbulent Priest

Holst became great friends with the local vicar, the socialist Father Conrad Noel, a colourful and controversial character who called him 'Our Mr Von'. Noel upset the villagers one day in 1921 by hoisting Sinn Fein and communist red flags above the church. To add fuel to the fire he deliberately omitted hoisting the Union Jack believing it to be a flag of imperialist oppression. Angry Cambridge students tore down the flags and replaced them with the Union Jack, an act which drove the vicar quite wild. A pitched battle ensued with Noel and his followers slashing the tyres of the demonstrators' cars and motorbikes until order was fully restored by the church authorities.

Summer Music Festival
In calmer times Holst played the church organ, helped local singers and brought London students to the parish church where they sang Bach cantatas and Byrd's *Mass for Three Voices*. At Christmas he sang carols and invited the choir to his home at the Manse in Town Street, where a plaque commemorates his residence here from 1917 to 1925. Holst died in 1934 and today he is remembered with a month-long summer music festival in Thaxted, which attracts performers worldwide.

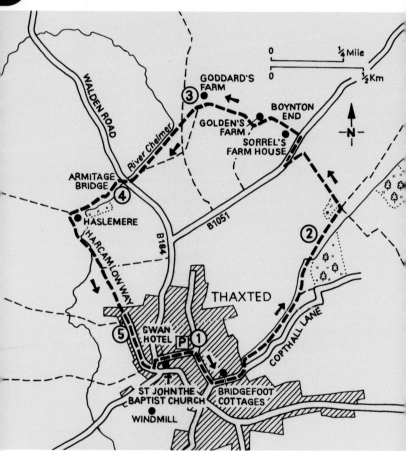

Walk 32 Directions

① From the car park turn left into **Margaret Street**, right into **Weaverhead Lane** and left into

Copthall Lane, passing the row of cottages called **Bridgefoot**. After the houses on your left, pass through the gap between trees by the gate marked Walnut Tree Meadow. Turn right along the grassy path and keep

Walk 32

parallel with Copthall Lane on your right. After 400yds (366m) bear left at the yellow waymark through trees, cross two footbridges at right angles, in quick succession, and turn right keeping the stream and hedgerows on your right.

② Maintain direction along the field-edge path through two fields. After the line of trees on your left, turn left at the waymark over the footbridge and follow another field-edge path keeping the hedgerow on your left to the **B1051**, Sampford road. In the distance, to your left, the spire of St John the Baptist Church dominates the skyline. Turn right, cross the road with care,and take the first turning on the left along the farm track marked **Boynton End**. The track zig-zags left and right past **Sorrel's Farm House** and **Golden Farm**. At Golden Farm bear right on to the narrow canopied bridleway between buildings, keeping the paddock

fence on your left. Continue downhill to the collection of waymarks outside **Goddards Farm**, turn left and right and follow the path uphill with the farm on your right-hand side.

③ Descend a short steep embankment and cross the farm track to follow a fingerpost through the hedge. Turn half left across the field and follow the path with the River Chelmer on your right to **Walden Road**.

④ At **Walden Road** turn right across **Armitage Bridge** and immediately left at the fingerpost. Follow the field-edge path with the river on your left passing conifers and, after 300yds (274m) where the river veers away, turn left at the waymark concealed in the hedgerows. You are now on the **Harcamlow Way**. Turn left downhill past the house called **Haslemere**, over the concrete bridge across the river. Ignore paths left and right and continue along the tarmac road, past some elegant modern housing surrounded by rolling countryside.

⑤ Continue along **Watling Lane** passing 17th-century cottages and Piggots Mill until you emerge opposite the **Swan Hotel**. Turn left and right into **Margaret Street** and return to the car park.

Walk 33

From Saffron Walden

A fairly challenging walk along part of the Harcamlow Way to Audley End, taking in beautiful rolling countryside.

•DISTANCE•	5½ miles (8.8km)
•MINIMUM TIME•	2hrs 30min
•ASCENT / GRADIENT•	180ft (55m) ▲▲▲
•LEVEL OF DIFFICULTY•	👫 👫 👫
•PATHS•	Urban, field edge, grassy tracks
•LANDSCAPE•	Downland, arable farmland, grassy meadow and woodland
•SUGGESTED MAP•	aqua3 OS Explorer 195 Braintree & Saffron Walden
•START / FINISH•	Grid reference: TL 534384
•DOG FRIENDLINESS•	Mostly on lead
•PARKING•	Pay-and-display at Swan Meadows, Common Hill and Fairycroft Road, free parking at Catons Hill
•PUBLIC TOILETS•	Swan Meadows, Common Hill and Hill Street

BACKGROUND TO THE WALK

Saffron Walden is a picturesque medieval town. Originally known as Walden meaning 'valley of the Welsh' (ie Britons), the town's distinctive prefix was added in the 15th century when many parts of north west Essex began growing the saffron crocus and the town became a centre of trade for saffron. Every autumn the flowers were picked by hand and brought to the town where the chive, or stigma, was removed, dried and then sold.

Saffron was mainly used for dyeing although a few Waldenians seem to have used it as a spice or medicine. By the early 1700s saffron production fell into decline mainly due to cheaper imports from Spain and the Middle East. However, the saffron flower symbol can be seen on the decorative plasterwork, or pargetting, on the Old Sun Inn in Church Street, inside the parish church and on the coat-of-arms on the Town Hall.

On this walk you can imagine what the surrounding countryside to the west of Saffron Walden must have looked like when it was covered with crocus blooms. We leave the town passing the Edward VI almshouses (1834), which provided homes for the poor, and walk along Abbey Lane to enter the wrought iron gates of Audley End Park. This great park extends from Saffron Walden to the Cambridge road and Audley End House, which stands on the site of the former Benedictine monastery of Walden Abbey.

Historic House and Fine Parkland

Audley End House was given to Sir Thomas Audley in 1538 by Henry VIII. It was used as a private residence but demolished and rebuilt by his grandson, Thomas Howard, 1st Earl of Suffolk, as a much grander mansion for entertaining James I. A story tells that Thomas Howard lied to the King saying he had spent £200,000 on creating the house and that the King had unwittingly contributed to the cost. In 1619 both Howard and his wife were locked up in the Tower of London for fraud but payment of a huge fine set them free and seven years later, Howard died in disgrace at Audley End. Today the house is a third of its original size but it is still very grand. We pass through the one-street hamlet of Audley End and its row of cottages, where the estate workers lived, before returning to town.

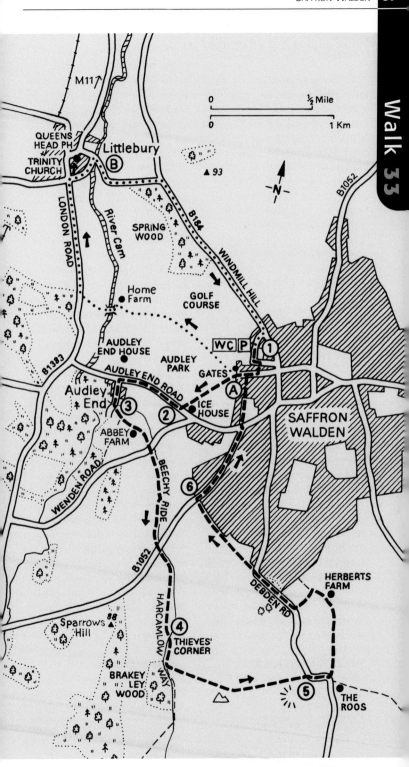

M11

QUEENS
HEAD PH
TRINITY
CHURCH
Littlebury
B

0   ½ Mile
0   1 Km

▲ 93

N

LONDON ROAD

River Cam

SPRING
WOOD

B184

WINDMILL HILL

Home
Farm

GOLF
COURSE

B1052

AUDLEY
END HOUSE

AUDLEY
PARK

WC P
①

B1383

AUDLEY END ROAD

GATES

Audley
End
③

②

ICE
HOUSE

A

SAFFRON
WALDEN

ABBEY
FARM

WENDEN ROAD

BEECHY RIDE

⑥

B1052

HARCAMLOW WAY

HERBERTS
FARM

DEBDEN RD

Sparrows
Hill

88
▲

④

THIEVES'
CORNER

⑤

THE
ROOS

BRAKEY
LEY
WOOD

△

Walk 33

Walk 33 Directions

① From the car park turn right into **Park Lane** and first right into **Primes Close**. Go through the arch under the almshouses and go right into **Abbey Lane** through the wrought iron gates of **Audley End Park**. Maintain direction along the grassy path to the top of the hill, passing the **Ice House** on your left by another set of wrought iron gates, to **Audley End Road**.

WHERE TO EAT AND DRINK ⓘ

Behind the post office, the **former schoolhouse**, at Audley End Village, is a tiny tea room which serves cakes, pastries and sandwiches. For a pub lunch head for the **Queens Head** at Littlebury. If visiting **Audley End House** try the cafeteria/restaurant.

---

② Turn right along the embankment and go downhill for 600yds (549m), keeping the red brick wall of Audley End Park on your right, until you reach the fingerpost marked **College of St Mark**. Cross the road and turn left to **Audley End** village.

③ Cross the bridge and turn left at the lane marked 'Abbey Farm private' and continue along this footpath keeping St Mark's College, followed by the farm, to your right. Maintain direction through arable fields, cross **Wenden Road** and go through trees to join **Beechy Ride** (track). Keep the stream and line of

beech trees to your right for 200yds (183m), until you cross the earth bridge between the trees, and continue with the stream and trees to your left to the **B1052**. Cross the road with care, turn right and continue until you reach a footpath on your left. Turn left along the field-edge path with the hedgerow and stream on your left. At the earth bridge turn left and immediately right so that the stream is now on your right.

④ Follow the field-edge path until it abuts **Brakey Ley Wood** and ignore three sets of waymarks indicating right turns. At the fourth waymark, **Thieves' Corner**, turn left just before the footbridge and follow the grassy field-edge path steeply uphill to **Debden Road**.

⑤ Turn right at Debden Road and opposite **The Roos**, turn left on to the uphill path. Bear left at **Herberts Farm** and left again to rejoin Debden Road. Turn right towards **Claypits Plantation** and maintain direction into **Seven Devil's Lane**.

⑥ After ½ mile (800m) turn right on the **B1052** towards **Saffron Walden**. At the roundabout bear left across the road and follow the footpath between houses passing a deep ditch on the left, which is part of ancient defence system called Battle Ditches. At the end of the path turn right into **Abbey Lane** and the car park.

WHILE YOU'RE THERE ⓘ

Don't miss a visit to **Audley End House**, an historic treasure trove of art and interior design. Run by English Heritage, the attractions include paintings by Holbein and Canaletto and a collection of 1,000 stuffed birds and animals.

WHAT TO LOOK FOR

Trinity Church at Littlebury has a 14th-century tower, a Norman nave and 13th-century aisles. Inside the church, look for the attractive brasses depicting local people, including several who died of the plague in 1522.

Around Audley End

A short loop walk from Audley End Park via Littlebury to Saffron Walden.
See map and information panel for Walk 33

Walk 34

•DISTANCE•	3 miles (4.8km)
•MINIMUM TIME•	1hr 15min
•ASCENT / GRADIENT•	123ft (37m)
•LEVEL OF DIFFICULTY•	

Walk 34 Directions (Walk 33 option)

After passing through the entrance gate to **Audley Park**, Point Ⓐ, turn right on to the path and after 200yds (183m) cross the footbridge and maintain direction uphill, with the stream and golf course on your right. Look to your left for views of Audley End House before reaching the Tudor brickwork stables roofs.

Audley End House dates back to the early 17th century when it was much grander than the mansion we see today. Part of it was demolished because successive owners couldn't afford its upkeep. In the 18th century Lord Braybrook ordered its refurbishment by the architect Vanbrugh. Robert Adam was the interior designer and 'Capability' Brown was the landscape genius.

At the farm track, turn left and cross two bridges over the **River Cam** and continue uphill to the **B1383**. Turn right and walk along the verge towards **Littlebury** for ½ mile (800m). Turn right into **Mill Lane**, passing **Trinity Church** on your left, followed by weatherboarded cottages and a converted mill, to the T-junction, Point Ⓑ.

Littlebury's claim to fame is the joke house built by Henry Winstanley, who also built Eddystone Lighthouse in 1698. He was born in Saffron Walden in 1644 and died in his own lighthouse in 1703. Winstanley lived near Trinity Church and would subject his houseguests to practical jokes, which included getting them to use a joke armchair, which wouldn't allow the sitter to get up.

Turn right into **Walden Road** and cross **Littlebury Bridge** over the River Cam. After 500yds (457m), turn right on to the **B184**, Windmill Hill. This is a busy road into Saffron Walden and the site of a Bronze Age settlement. You can walk safely along the raised embankment passing the flint walls of **Spring Wood** on your right. Walk for ¾ mile (1.2km) and turn right into **New Pond Lane** passing Saffron Walden Golf Club to return to **Swan Meadows** car park.

WHAT TO LOOK FOR ⓘ

Swan Meadows was a swampy place and legend has it that a serpent once lurked here and killed half the local population. It was left as overgrown grassland and became a rare wet pasture habitat for birds. Scandalously, it was converted into a car park in 1992, but some nature thrives in the nearby pond.

Saffron Walden Town

A stroll taking in the architectural splendours of a country market town.

•DISTANCE•	3½ miles (5.7km)
•MINIMUM TIME•	1hr 30 min
•ASCENT / GRADIENT•	62ft (19m) ▲ ▲ ▲
•LEVEL OF DIFFICULTY•	🚶 🚶 🚶
•PATHS•	Urban, parkland and common
•LANDSCAPE•	Country town architecture
•SUGGESTED MAP•	aqua3 OS Explorer 195 Braintree & Saffron Walden
•START / FINISH•	Grid reference: TL 540385
•DOG FRIENDLINESS•	On lead all the way, though maze is dog friendly
•PARKING•	Pay-and-display at Swan Meadows, Common Hill and Fairycroft Road, free parking at Catons Hill
•PUBLIC TOILETS•	Swan Meadows, Common Hill and Hill Street

Walk 35 **Directions**

Saffron Walden is a delightful country town and well worth a visit at any time of the year. In 1968, it was designated a Conservation Area, unsurprising perhaps when you consider that the town has some 400 buildings of special architectural or historic interest dating back to medieval times. There are houses with massive timbers, carved brackets, overhanging eaves and plastered decorative fronts, or pargetting, and a fine church looks boldly across the town. Other attractions include two mazes and lovely gardens, the remains of a Norman castle and

> **WHILE YOU'RE THERE** ⓘ
> The **museum**, which opened in 1835 as a natural history museum, lies adjacent to the ruins of Saffron Walden's 12th-century castle. It has superb displays of local history including galleries on architecture, costume, pottery and a Discovery Centre highlighting the nature and wildlife of north west Essex.

some great walking country right on its doorstep. This trail explores part of the Conservation Area but you should allow time to wander at will and lap up the atmosphere of this picturesque town.

With your back to **Common Hill** car park walk across **The Common** to **The Maze**. The Common, formerly Castle Green, which played host to a Royal Tournament in 1252, is nowadays a pleasant recreational venue for local fairs and festivals. At the far end is The Maze, believed to be over 800 years old and reputed to be the largest turf maze in the country. If you have time you can enjoy exploring its mile-length trail before continuing the town walk.

At **The Maze**, turn right to the river and right again, keeping the river on your left to head back to the car park. At the car park turn left then right into **Hill Street**, turn right into **Market Street** passing Market Row on your left into **Market Square**. This is the hub of the town.

The mock-Tudor Town Hall, with a projecting gable, houses the tourist office. Other notable buildings include the Italianate-style Corn Exchange, now the library, and an impressive drinking fountain commemorating the marriage between the Prince of Wales and Princess Alexandra in 1863.

> ### WHAT TO LOOK FOR ⓘ
> Look for the **weavers' cottages** in town and imagine the sound of clattering looms behind closed doors during the height of the wool industry. In Gold Street there are 17th-century cottages which have a communal rear courtyard.

Keeping the **Corn Exchange** on your left, walk towards **Museum Street** (at the junction with **Church Street**) to the historic **Sun Inn** where Cromwell is said to have stayed during the Civil War. On the corner there is a group of 14th-century houses decorated with impressive 17th-century pargetting. Turn left into **Church Street** and right into the churchyard of **St Mary the Virgin**.

St Mary the Virgin, with its saffron crocus emblem, is one of the largest parish churches in the county. Standing on the site of a Saxon and Norman church it was mostly rebuilt between 1450 and 1525 and its sheer size demonstrates the prosperity of the area.

At the church, turn right, cross **Museum Street** to view the museum and the ruined flint walls of the 11th-century castle keep, built on the remains of a Saxon church. Retrace your steps to **Museum Street**, turn right and then left into **Castle Street**. After 350yds (320m), turn right into **Bridge End Gardens** and the town's other maze.

These gardens exude early Victorian elegance with a viewing platform, pavilions and statues.

Take the main path left into **Bridge Street**. Turn left to pass the 16th-century **Eight Bells** pub, with its fine carved beam decorated with leaves and dolphins below the downstairs middle window. Maintain direction towards the town crossing **Castle Street**, where on the right you can see the finest 15th-century medieval building in Saffron Walden. A former maltings, and one of six which graced the town in the 1600s, it's now the Youth Hostel and must be one of the most atmospheric places to stay in the county. On the left is the 16th-century house called The Close, home of Francis Gibson, creator of Bridge End Gardens.

Continue along **Bridge Street** to see more listed buildings. These include the Army and Navy Stores, a good example of a 16th-century house with original first floor windows. Another 16th-century architectural masterpiece is the **Cross Keys Hotel**, with a raised roof which was added in the 18th century. Turn left into **King Street** and right in front of Dobsons and The Hoops. These buildings still retain their 15th-century shop windows. Go left into **Market Row** to return to the car park.

> ### WHERE TO EAT AND DRINK ⓘ
> There are plenty of pubs, restaurants, coffee shops and take-aways to choose from. The **Kings Arms**, a cosy pub dating back to Tudor times in the heart of the town, is a good place for home-cooked food and real ales. The **Mocha Café & Diner** in Central Arcade offers a wide choice of meals, snacks and sandwiches and has a take-away service too.

Walk 36

Lambourne End to Chigwell

A challenging walk combining an ancient forest, a village immortalised by Dickens and panoramic views of the London skyline.

•DISTANCE•	9 miles (14.5km)
•MINIMUM TIME•	3hrs 30 min
•ASCENT / GRADIENT•	148ft (45m) ▲▲▲
•LEVEL OF DIFFICULTY•	🚶 🚶 🚶
•PATHS•	Forest tracks, field-edge paths, green lanes, some streets, 9 stiles
•LANDSCAPE•	Forest, meadows, fields and some urban streets
•SUGGESTED MAP•	aqua3 OS Explorer 174 Epping Forest & Lee Valley
•START / FINISH•	Grid reference: TQ 478943
•DOG FRIENDLINESS•	Lots of big stiles, but water bowl at Kings Head
•PARKING•	Three free car parks along Manor Road in Hainault Forest
•PUBLIC TOILETS•	Hainault Forest Country Park visitors' centre (not on route)

BACKGROUND TO THE WALK

Hainault Forest was once part of the royal forest which stretched right across Essex. Like the forests of Epping and Hatfield, deer were bred here to supply the royal table, but the forest is also famous for being the stamping ground of a rather infamous character, Dick Turpin (1705–39). This legendary highwayman probably had a hand in the business of poaching deer and whatever else he could lay his hands on, before turning his talents to the less risky pursuits of housebreaking and robbery.

A Life of Crime

Born in a pub in Hempstead, the young Dick started his working life as a butcher in Whitechapel. One day, when caught in the act of cattle rustling, he fled to deepest Essex, only to resurface as a small-time smuggler, thief and highwayman. The business of travel in Turpin's time was no mean feat, for who knew when he or his cronies would strike as those brave enough made the dangerous journey through Hainault Forest? When a job was done, Turpin would call at Ye Old Kings Head in Chigwell for a quick pint, pick up details of when the next coach was due and plan his next crime. After a life of highway robbery and murder he was hung at York, but it was thanks to Harrison Ainsworth's novel, *Rookwood* (1834), in which a description of his supposed epic ride from Westminster to York caught the popular imagination, that Turpin was transformed into a glamorous character.

In the forest it is not difficult to picture a masked highwayman galloping through misty woodlands of weirdly sculpted trees to Chigwell Row, with its delightful church and collection of characterful hostelries. In the area around east London there are many pubs called the Black Horse in honour of Turpin's steed, Black Bess, but it is at Ye Old Kings Head at Chigwell where, it is said, the rogue secreted his pistols inside the walls. They have not been found, neither has the cellar tunnel connected to Chigwell church across the road, which he used to escaped his pursuers.

Relish the atmosphere of this old Tudor pub which Charles Dickens (1812-70) described as the Maypole (not to be confused with the Maypole at Chigwell Row) in

Barnaby Rudge (1841). Of Ye Old Kings Head he wrote that it had 'more gable-ends than a lazy man would care to count on a sunny day'. As you walk across the rolling countryside, particularly between Chigwell and Lambourne End, a superb London skyline with Canary Wharf in the distance reveals itself. And although it's said that the ghost of Dick Turpin riding Black Bess appears twice a week, he won't trouble you as long as you keep to the marked paths…

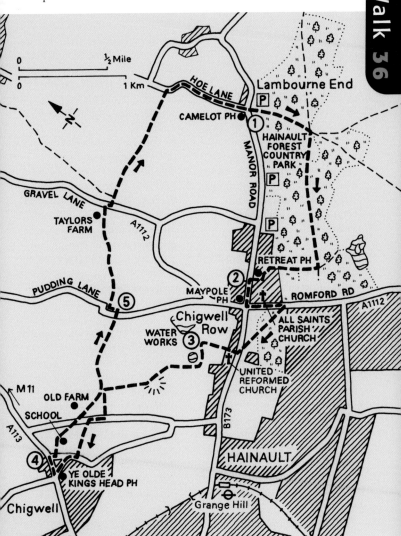

Walk 36 Directions

① From the car park walk straight along the wide bridleway between high trees. There is little forest floor covering and to the left you can see deep ancient woodland. After 350yds (320m) at the three-way fingerpost, turn right on to footpath **No 43** towards **Hainault**. This stone chipping path runs

Walk 36

parallel with the bridleway on your left. At the second fingerpost go right for **Retreat Path**. This wide bridleway has many coppiced and pollarded oaks and hornbeams. After 300yds (320m), bear left to pass the backs of houses on your left. Maintain your direction through the kissing gate to the **Retreat** pub car park.

② Turn left into **Manor Road** and, at traffic lights, turn left for **All Saints Church**. Cross **Romford Road** and bear right on the cross-field path through the recreation ground. Cross **Manor Road** and into **Chapel Lane** passing the United Reformed church on your left. Take the narrow path between houses to the small meadow.

③ Maintain direction across four stiles and at the iron fence turn left along the path, keeping the waterworks behind the fencing to your right. At the concrete path at the waterworks gate, bear half left.

At the break in the hedgerow on your left there are views of rolling countryside. Follow the field-edge path downhill, keeping the hedgerow on your right, to the fingerpost. Turn left and continue along the field-edge path. Turn right on to the green lane and walk uphill with the Old Farm buildings to the right. Just before **Old Farm** turn left across a field, turn right and cross **Vicarage Lane**. After 150yds (146m) turn left on the path emerging on **Chigwell High Road**.

④ Turn right and right again, back into **Vicarage Lane**. Turn immediately left on to the cross-field path. Then bear right passing the primary school on your right. Follow the fingerpost diagonally across two fields, and maintain direction downhill crossing two stiles and the footbridge. Turn left and left again through the hedgerow then right, on to the field-edge path uphill.

⑤ At the top, cross **Pudding Lane** and follow the fingerpost on the field-edge path keeping Pudding Lane on your left. Take the cross-field path right and emerge by **Taylor's Farm**. Cross **Gravel Lane** beside Taylor's Farm gate and continue uphill towards a dead tree, passing through the gap in the hedge to the right. Maintain direction to **Hoe Lane** and turn right to return to the car park.

Old and New Come Together at Harlow

A leisurely stroll exploring town and country from Mark Hall to Old Harlow.

•DISTANCE•	4 miles (6.4km)
•MINIMUM TIME•	1hr 30min
•ASCENT / GRADIENT•	67ft (20m) ▲▲ ▲ ▲
•LEVEL OF DIFFICULTY•	🚶 🚶 🚶
•PATHS•	Cycle tracks, footpaths, sections of road, 1 stile
•LANDSCAPE•	Urban, undulating farmland dotted with woodland
•SUGGESTED MAP•	aqua3 OS Explorer 174 Epping Forest & Lee Valley
•START / FINISH•	Grid reference: TL 465109
•DOG FRIENDLINESS•	Mainly on lead but can stretch legs in meadows and good welcome at pubs
•PARKING•	Free car park at Harlow Museum open Tuesday to Sunday. Otherwise plenty of on-street parking
•PUBLIC TOILETS•	Harlow Museum

BACKGROUND TO THE WALK

In 1944 Harlow was one of 32 locations around London selected as a site for a new town. On the western edge of Essex, the area consisted of a few scattered hamlets and farms and, apart from the villages of Old Harlow and Potter Street, it was rural and undeveloped with many fine trees and woodlands. Although close to London, Harlow was never intended to be a satellite of the capital, but a self-contained town with its own amenities to house Londoners whose homes had been destroyed in World War Two.

A Network of Cycle Tracks

Eminent architect Sir Frederick Gibberd proposed that the new town should be just west of the original village of Old Harlow. It was to consist of a central civic area surrounded by four large neighbourhood clusters, each with its own shops, churches, library, medical and community centres and schools. The clusters would be separated by wide green areas carrying the town's main roads. The woodland areas were increased by planting many thousands of trees, thus enhancing Harlow's rural atmosphere. In and around Harlow you will discover an independent system of cycle tracks, some former medieval lanes, which conserve the landscape and provide a link with the past.

A New Museum

This walk starts from Mark Hall North, the first residential area to be built by Sir Frederick in 1953, and continues to the rural setting of Old Harlow, Mulberry and Churchgate Street in the east. In the 1950s many people cycled to work and these lanes are pedestrian-friendly, including the one we take near the Museum of Harlow, which is an extension of the original lane running from the centre of the new town to Old Harlow. Many old buildings nestle happily alongside the modern housing developments and the countryside reaches right into the centre thus earning its 'green town' reputation. On this route you will see Old Harlow, walk through the site of a Roman settlement, now a recreational park, and pass the medieval chapel of Harlowbury before reaching Churchgate Street with its delightful church and pubs backed by rural landscapes.

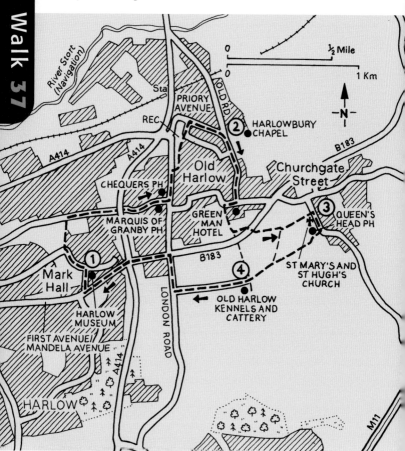

Walk 37 Directions

① Turn right outside **Harlow Museum**, take the first left into **Muskham Road** and follow the fingerpost to join the cycle path called **Netteswell Road**. Turn right and follow the cycle path under the A414 and into **Old Harlow**. Continue along **Market Street** to the T-junction and turn left at the **Chequers** pub into **Station Road**. After 300yds (274m), turn right

into the **Swallows Estate**, take the first left and follow the footpath through the recreational park to **Manor Road**. Turn left then right into **Priory Avenue** passing a row of corporation houses, the first to be built in the early days of Harlow new town, until you come to the crossroads with **Old Road**.

② Turn right and to your left you can just see 12th-century Harlowbury Chapel worked in flint and rubble, but for better views

Walk 37

walk another 150yds (137m) along Old Road to the kissing gate. Maintain direction until you reach the T-junction opposite the **Green Man Hotel**. Here turn right and take the footpath between the old ambulance and fire station and walk the field-edge path. Just before the main road, turn left between concrete posts and follow the footpath to the **B183**. Bear half left, cross the road and follow the footpath through trees and bear left on to the field-edge path. After 200yds (183m), cross the stile and the footbridge and walk towards the spire of **St Mary's and St Hugh's Church** and arrive at the graveyard.

③ Turn right into **Churchgate Street** passing the 17th-century Widow's House – inscribed with a dedication by a landowner's wife to a pair of poor widows – followed by the **Queen's Head** pub and other timber-framed houses. Continue downhill for 200yds (183m) to the footpath on the right just before **Churchgate Manor Hotel**. Keeping

> **WHERE TO EAT AND DRINK** ⓘ
> Fine old pubs with plenty of atmosphere include the **Chequers**, the **Marquis of Granby** and the **Green Man Hotel** in Old Harlow, and the **Queens Head** in Churchgate Street, a 16th-century house first used as an inn in the 18th century. All serve a range of hot and cold food.

the church and stream on your right, follow the field-edge path to the kissing gate. Bear half left across the meadow through the break in the fence opposite and, keeping the trees on your right, continue to the kissing gate at the top of the hill.

④ Pass the outbuildings of the Old Harlow Kennels and Cattery on your left and follow the tarmac road to **London Road**. Turn right into London Road and cross just before the roundabout on to the **B183** to the next roundabout on the **A414**. Follow the underpass into **First Avenue/Mandela Avenue**, turn left and take the first right back to **Harlow Museum**.

> **WHAT TO LOOK FOR** ⓘ
> Visit the brand new **Museum of Harlow** which tells the story of Harlow from prehistoric times to the present day. It includes a gallery of bicycles, a local history library and has an access point for the Essex Record Office. The former 19th-century stable block and walled garden is adjacent to Mark Hall, once owned by the influential Arkwright family from 1819 until fire destroyed all but one wing in 1947.

> **WHILE YOU'RE THERE** ⓘ
> Stroll round the grounds of **Harlow Study Centre**, an educational establishment, at Netteswellbury. At this former farm complex you can see the 13th-century St Andrew's Church beside two fine medieval tithe barns which were linked to Waltham Abbey, a walled garden and manor house. The buildings follow the layout of the original farm and house the kitchen, stores and office. They are surrounded by sheltered housing and are a classic example of how modern developments can blend with historic buildings.

26/02/06

Matching the Villages

A walk between Matching Tye and Matching Green with a church to match.

Walk 38

•DISTANCE•	3½ miles (5.7km)
•MINIMUM TIME•	1hr 30min
•ASCENT / GRADIENT•	Negligible
•LEVEL OF DIFFICULTY•	
•PATHS•	Bridleways, grass and field-edge paths, 3 stiles
•LANDSCAPE•	Ponds, patches of woodland and grassy meadow
•SUGGESTED MAP•	aqua3 OS Explorer 183 Chelmsford & The Rodings, Maldon & Witham
•START / FINISH•	Grid reference: TL 515112
•DOG FRIENDLINESS•	Notices everywhere warn of grazing stock
•PARKING•	Free parking at Matching Tye village hall
•PUBLIC TOILETS•	None on route

BACKGROUND TO THE WALK

You sometimes feel that Essex place names were designed to disorientate and confuse. Either that, or a Saxon cartographer got it all wrong when three tiny villages which form a triangle to the east of Harlow were named Matching Tye, Matching Green and Matching. Matching itself is the oldest of the trio and has changed little since Saxon times when the Maecca or Match people settled in what was then open forest. After the 5th century, this community expanded into Matching Tye and Matching Green.

Take in Two Trails
In this walk we shall discover the flint-and-rubble Church of St Mary the Virgin, built in 1200 over the site of an original Saxon church at Matching. The church stands in an atmosphere of pastoral peace, while next to it is the recently restored Marriage Feast House. A generous Mr William Chimney built the Feast House in 1480 and allowed local brides and grooms to celebrate their happy day there, a tradition that continued right up until 1936. The large oak tree beside the church was planted to celebrate Queen Victoria's Diamond Jubilee in 1887. These days the Feast House is used as an annexe for church activities. Near by there is a splendid lake filled with waterfowl, a lovely 15th-century timber-framed manor house surrounded by a water-filled moat and a large aisled barn dating back to the 1600s.

Matching Green, to the south east of Matching, is another village barely touched by time save for a picturesque collection of 18th-century weather-boarded cottages overlooking the green. There used to be some shops and half a dozen pubs, but nowadays it is a quiet spot where local people down a pint at the village's only surviving pub, the Chequers. The celebrated portrait artist, Augustus John (1878–1961), whose subjects included Thomas Hardy and George Bernard Shaw, lived in Elm House, next door.

The third village in this trio is Matching Tye renowned for its attractive Conservation Area of historic dwellings clustered round the tiny green. As you wander through the village you'll see a range of building materials used which include weather-boarding, yellow stock and red brick, red plain clay tiles, slate and thatch. The oldest buildings are the 16th-century Ployters Farm and Little Brewers, just before reaching your journey's end at the Fox Inn.

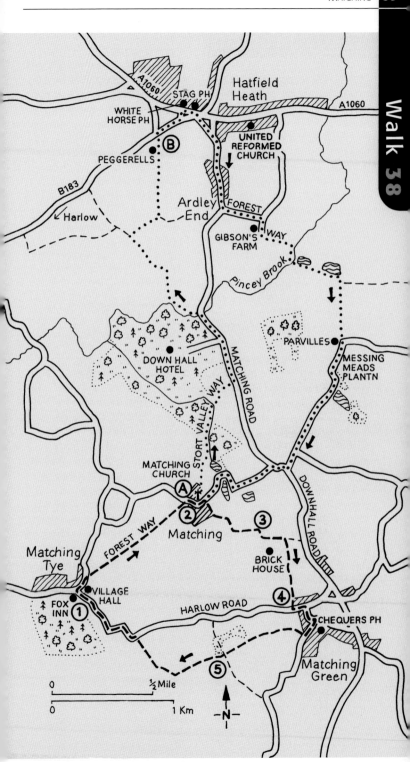

Walk 38 Directions

① From **Matching Tye village hall** turn right. Directly opposite the Fox Inn take the lane, signposted for **Sheering** and **Hatfield Heath**. After 200yds (183m), turn right at the fingerpost for the **Forest Way** and follow the grassy field-edge path. Go through the wooden gate and maintain direction along the bridleway to **Matching church**.

② Pass the **Marriage Feast House** on your left and continue to the metalled road to the right of the church. Take the footpath on your right, opposite the church, through the kissing gate and skirt the moat on your right. After 100yds (91m), cross the stile and walk half left on the cross-field path towards the edge of the line of trees. At the yellow waymark, turn left along the cross-field path.

③ At the mid-field fingerpost, turn right and walk to the line of trees, which is the boundary of **Brick House**. Turn left at the fingerpost, keeping the house and paddock on your right. After the paddock turn right across the field towards houses, maintain direction along the field-edge path. After the playing field on your left, walk between houses into **Harlow Road** at **Matching Green**.

④ Turn left and immediately right, following the signpost for **Epping**, and take the first right into **Colvers**. After 200yds (183m), turn right at the break in the hedge and go over two stiles in quick succession. Cross the meadow and maintain direction over the footbridge. Take the cross-field path half left towards the line of trees. Keep the trees on your right passing the yellow waymark to another copse of trees.

> ### WHERE TO EAT AND DRINK ⓘ
> Two fine watering holes with plenty of character on this route include the **Fox Inn** at Matching Tye and the **Chequers** at Matching Green. Both have car parks and serve home-cooked hot and cold meals, and a good selection of beer, wine and soft drinks. Otherwise try the upmarket **Down Hall Hotel**.

⑤ Maintain a south westerly direction and, soon after the footpath appears on your left, bear right on the field-edge path keeping the ditch and trees on your right-hand side. After about 100yds (91m), turn left then right through the trees and walk for 300yds (274m) with the trees on your right until you reach **Harlow Road**. Turn left and walk with care along the busy Harlow Road for around ½ mile (800m) to return to the village hall at **Matching Tye**. Here you can finish off with a well-earned rest at the nearby comfortable **Fox Inn**.

> ### WHILE YOU'RE THERE ⓘ
> **Down Hall** stands on the site of a Tudor farmhouse, which was demolished in the 18th century. It was rebuilt in 1870 in classical style and is noted for its Italianate design. A once grand private residence, it became a military hospital during World War One, and then a girls' school and management training centre before becoming a hotel in 1986.

> ### WHAT TO LOOK FOR ⓘ
> During World War Two American airmen and their engineers were based at **Matching Airfield**. Most of the land has now been reclaimed and only the control tower and radar building remain, but you can look for the memorial, erected to those who never returned, to the east of Matching Green.

A Hike to Hatfield Heath

A longer loop walk from Matching takes you to Hatfield Heath.
See map and information panel for Walk 38

•DISTANCE•	6 miles (9.7km)
•MINIMUM TIME•	3hrs
•ASCENT / GRADIENT•	90ft (27m) ▲▲▲
•LEVEL OF DIFFICULTY•	🚶🚶 🚶🚶 🚶🚶

Walk 39 Directions (Walk 38 option)

From **Matching** you can continue to **Hatfield Heath** on the **Stort Valley Way**. Go through the graveyard at **Matching church**, Point Ⓐ, to the kissing gate. Bear right downhill to cross the footbridge and bear right following the waymark to the stile. Cross the stile, follow the embankment to the end and turn right along the field-edge path. At the next fingerpost turn right over the stile, turn left keeping the stream on your right for 200yds (183m) and then bear right over the earth bridge. Follow the waymark for **Stort Valley Way**, cross another stile, follow the field-edge path until you turn left on to the **Matching road**. Pass **Down Hall Hotel** and turn left on to the waymarked field-edge path keeping **Pincey Brook** on your left. Follow the narrow waymarked path to **Peggerells**. Maintain direction until you reach the road via two wooden doors at the sides of houses, Point Ⓑ. Turn right to **Hatfield Heath**, always a quiet backwater of its more well-to-do neighbour, Hatfield Broad Oak.

With your back to the **Stag** take the tarmac road to **Ardley End**. Follow the signpost towards **Friar's Farm**, passing **Gibson's Farm** and lovely views of rolling countryside. You are now on the **Forest Way** and should follow these waymarks. Leave Gibson's Farm behind, turn left on to the field-edge path and, at the next waymark, turn right and at the footbridge, turn left.

Climb the steep embankment, pass two reservoirs on your left and turn right uphill to **Parvilles**, an isolated farmstead, near the site of the original 17th-century timber-framed farm building which was destroyed by fire in 1945.

Bear right on to the grassy embankment between oak trees and go downhill towards **Messing Meads Plantation**. Soon you see a third reservoir on your left, but maintain direction until you reach **Downhall Road**. Turn right and follow the sign to **Matching church** to rejoin Walk 38.

WHERE TO EAT AND DRINK ⓘ

Two delightful 18th-century pubs, the **White Horse** and the **Stag**, can be found at Hatfield Heath. The Stag serves tasty tuna sandwiches and tea and a good range of pub food. It's also dog friendly. Dogless walkers may like the offerings at the **Countryman Restaurant** next door to the Stag.

Walk 40

Hatfield Forest

Walk through part of the once extensive Royal Forest of Essex.

·DISTANCE·	4½ miles (7.2km)
·MINIMUM TIME·	2hrs
·ASCENT / GRADIENT·	89ft (27m) ▲ ▲ ▲
·LEVEL OF DIFFICULTY·	🚶 🚶 🚶
·PATHS·	Grassy paths and forest trails, 1 stile
·LANDSCAPE·	Ancient coppice woodland, meadows, lakes and marsh
·SUGGESTED MAP·	aqua3 OS Explorer 195 Braintree & Saffron Walden
·START / FINISH·	Grid reference: TL 546203
·DOG FRIENDLINESS·	Off-limits around part of lake; but main area dog friendly as long as on lead
·PARKING·	Pay-and-display car parks at main entrance and Shell House inside the forest. Exit gates close at 8PM
·PUBLIC TOILETS·	Beside Forest Café inside forest

Walk 40 Directions

In the 12th century Hatfield was under Crown ownership and deer were bred to supply the King's table. Nobody but the King and his cronies were allowed to hunt and hapless peasants, if caught killing animals in the forest might have their hands cut off, or worse still be executed. By 1446 the forest was owned by a succession of families, including Robert the Bruce, but the last owners from 1729 to 1923 were the Houblons, descendants of the founders of the Bank of England. Today sheep and cattle still graze on the open grassland, barely changed since Norman times, and you might catch a glimpse of shy fallow deer or the smaller Muntjac deer in the coppices.

From the car park follow the surfaced road for 350yds (320m) and at the concrete spur path bear half left across pastureland. After 250yds (229m), go through the wooden gate passing coppiced hornbeam woods to the lake on your right. Bear right for 70yds (64m), to cross the dam dividing the lake, home to many birds throughout the year, and follow the path to **Shell House**.

Shell House was built by the Houblons who lived at Hallingbury Place to the west of the forest, and created the lake in about 1746 by damming Shermore Brook. They bred peacocks, planted exotic trees and held grand lakeside picnics. In 1923 they sold the forest and for a while its future remained uncertain, especially when the new owner happened to be a timber merchant.

> **WHAT TO LOOK FOR** ℹ️
> Throughout the year the lake is home to many **birds**, including martins and swallows in spring, mallards and moorhens in summer and tufted ducks and pochards in winter. You'll also see typical features of a medieval forest in various mounds, ditches and banks built to keep livestock off grazing land.

Walk 40

Then naturalist Edward North Buxton came to the rescue writing out a cheque as part payment for the forest before he died. His sons completed the transaction and gave the forest to the National Trust.

Leave the car park at **Shell House**. Turn left and follow the path south, with the smaller lake on your left, to the wide grassy path until you reach a 'wantz', an Essex word for a junction where rides intersect. You are now at **Collins Coppice**. Turn right here, on to the wide grassy bridleway for 250yds (229m) and bear right on to the plain, making for **Forest Lodge** in the distance. Keeping the Lodge to your left-hand side, continue north on the wide plain passing **Warren Cottage** on your right.

Warren Cottage used to house the warrener, who in medieval times would look after the rabbit warren. Rabbits were introduced from Spain in the 12th century for food and fur. The remains of the warren are still visible in the form of pillow-shaped mounds behind the cottage.

Bear left across the wide grassy plain dotted with maple, ash and hawthorn. This was the former London Road, where stage coaches from East Anglia would cross the bridge over Shermore Brook. Keeping close to the woods on your left, continue north westwards for ½ mile (800m), until you meet a cross path. Turn right here, on to the **Flitch Way**.

The railway track, a casualty of Dr Beeching's cuts in 1969, formed part of the line linking Bishops Stortford and Braintree. Now the Flitch Way, this path buzzes with butterflies and birds in summer while slow worms, grass snakes and lizards make their homes on the south-facing banks. Continue for 500yds (457m) and, after the bridge, turn right along the path with Shermore Brook on your right. Many wild flowers grow in this damp area and you'll notice the pungently aromatic water mint and the bright yellow flowers of fleabane as you approach the footbridge. This is quite a marshy area and if you make a detour into **Dowsett's Coppice** on your left you will see oxlips and a plateau of alder trees.

Continue south and, just after the footbridge, turn left over the stile and into woodland. Follow the narrow path between coppiced trees to the confluence of paths known as **Eight Wantz**. Continue straight ahead on to the widest path to the next cross path and turn right along the path between the last of the coppiced trees, before emerging on to open grass land. Bear slightly right keeping trees of **Elgin Coppice** to your right. Cross the tarmac road and maintain direction back to the car park resplendent with the ancient pollarded trees which welcomed you at the beginning of the walk.

Pretty Ugley

An easy ramble taking in views of undulating countryside and part of the Harcamlow Way.

•DISTANCE•	5½ miles (8.8km)
•MINIMUM TIME•	2hrs 15min
•ASCENT / GRADIENT•	75ft (23m) ▲ ▲ ▲
•LEVEL OF DIFFICULTY•	🚶 🚶 🚶
•PATHS•	Woodland and grassy tracks, field edge, some road walking, 5 stiles
•LANDSCAPE•	Gently undulating arable and grazing farmland, some woodland and isolated farmsteads
•SUGGESTED MAP•	aqua3 OS Explorer 195 Braintree & Saffron Walden
•START / FINISH•	Grid reference: TL 513288
•DOG FRIENDLINESS•	Decent-sized field-edge paths and dog-friendly stiles make this walk hassle-free
•PARKING•	Free car park at Chequers pub, Cambridge Road
•PUBLIC TOILETS•	None on route

BACKGROUND TO THE WALK

Ugley village, straddling the busy Cambridge to London road and a few miles north of Stansted Mountfitchet, is the butt of many jokes. It's tempting not to start this walk without references to ugly people, ugly ducklings and ugly sisters, such descriptions of course being in the eye of the beholder. But it is nothing like the Cinderella of Essex villages and is, in fact, a pretty hamlet consisting of delightful houses, a pub, village hall, church and even an Ugley Womens Institute, although no members have yet entered the Ugley Beauty Competition! Walkers, on the other hand, will discover just one blot on the landscape and that is the black netting of the landfill site, visible for miles around, on this otherwise lovely walk through gently undulating countryside.

A Ghostly Tale

The village is named after Ugga the Viking who set up home in a clearing, or ley, in what was once a huge forest. Those forests have long since gone and today are replaced by arable farmland, patches of woodland, plantations of pine forests, isolated farmsteads and the tiny hamlets of Ugley and Ugley Green. Ghost stories are rife in Ugley and where better a place to start a spooky trail than from the Chequers pub. This 16th-century coaching inn stands near the site of a Viking burial ground and was almost in ruins when its present owner bought it some years ago. It's said that some parts of the pub are haunted and that if you linger long enough you can feel an inexplicably chilly draft. If you're extra vigilant you may see the ghost-like figure of a wizened Victorian lady dressed from head to toe in black. Some tradesmen swear they will not work in the pub unless there are plenty of people around.

From the pub we walk into the woods, now pine plantations, where Ugga and his friends may have set up camp, and continue on to the Harcamlow Way, part of a figure-of-eight 140 mile (225km) cross country route between Harlow and Cambridge. On the way you pass the dilapidated farmstead of Wade's Hall, with its outbuildings entwined in ivy and just the sort of place to spot Ugga's ghost. Bollington Hall, the next farmhouse, stands majestically on a hill overlooking gently undulating farmland and it is indeed a pleasure to walk along this landowner's wide field-edge paths with wonderful views of Ugley.

Our walk continues to Ugley Green where The Place, a magnificent thatched house, overlooks the green. A few miles across open fields brings us to Ugley Church where the Victorian lady in black sometimes hovers amidst the gravestones. Hurry on to the Chequers for some sustenance, but make sure you avoid sitting in that chilly draft…

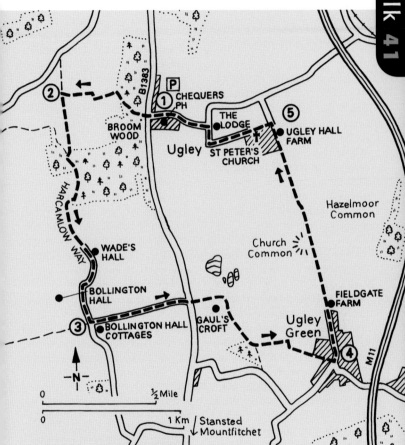

Walk 41 **Directions**

① Cross the **B1383** with care and follow the fingerpost directly opposite the **Chequers** through **Broom Wood**. Cross the stile and follow the yellow waymarks through the plantation of conifers, via the plank bridge and another stile. After the stile, turn left and

follow the field-edge path to the right. Maintain direction following the field-edge path right and left until you reach the cross path.

② Turn left on to the wide cross-field path towards conifers. Go through the gap in the hedgerow and left on the wide bridle path, which is the **Harcamlow Way**. Ignore the path left and bear right

Walk 41

WHERE TO EAT AND DRINK ⓘ

The lack of choice of eateries in the area is compensated by the variety of food at the **Chequers** pub in Cambridge Road, Ugley. This former 16th-century coaching inn has plenty of character, welcomes walkers and cyclists and has an attractive garden where you can relax with your dog. Choose from an extensive carnivorous and vegetarian menu or opt for tasty sandwiches or salads.

to continue along the Harcamlow Way south, with fields on your right and the conifer wood to your left. Maintain your direction passing the dilapidated farm buildings of **Wade's Hall**, followed by the isolated farmstead of **Bollington Hall**. From now on the path is tarmac, with arable fields on either side and clear views of the houses at **Ugley**.

③ Turn left in front of **Bollington Hall Cottages** and take the straight road towards the **B1383**, with the skyline of Ugley looming ahead. Cross the road with care and follow the narrow, overgrown path ahead through **Gaul's Croft**. This well-defined path crosses the stile and meanders through the small thick forest bounded by bramble. At the next waymark, bear half left along the field-edge path and continue via waymarks right and left between houses to emerge at peaceful **Ugley Green**. Stop for a breather here to

take in the architecture of elegant houses from various periods, some of which are thatched.

④ Turn left along the tarmac road following the '**Fieldgate Lane no-through road**' sign. Maintain direction past houses, passing the modern looking **Fieldgate Farm** on your right. The road becomes a wide muddy track bisecting arable fields and from this high elevation there are views to the west of Bollington Hall, the tranquillity of which is broken by the noisy traffic on the M11 ½ mile (800m) away.

⑤ The track bisects the outbuildings of **Ugley Hall Farm** where you maintain direction on to the road and turn left immediately after the large corrugated barn and into **St Peter's Church** at Ugley. Go through the churchyard and follow the tarmac road through grazing fields, passing **The Lodge**, where you turn left and return via **Patmore End** to the car park.

WHILE YOU'RE THERE ⓘ

Look for the **32nd milestone** from London on the Cambridge Road, famous amongst cycling enthusiasts of all ages. It is just north of the Chequers pub and is the start and finishing point of many cycling trials. You may see members of the 32nd Association (or their ghosts!) formed from various clubs throughout Essex who make regular use of this road.

WHAT TO LOOK FOR ⓘ

Ugley Green has a clutch of beautiful thatched houses overlooking the green. If you cross the green and walk towards the bus stop you will see a perfectly preserved water pump beside a huge pudding stone. **Pudding stones** are glacial deposits dating back 180 million years and look like a boiled suet pudding studded with cherries and currants. Pilgrims would use them as medieval markers in much the same way as we use fingerposts and road signs.

Walk 42

Taking Off from Stansted

A rural walk beside the runway of London's third international airport and a plane spotter's paradise.

•DISTANCE•	3¼ miles (5.3km)
•MINIMUM TIME•	1hr 30min
•ASCENT / GRADIENT•	54ft (16m)
•LEVEL OF DIFFICULTY•	
•PATHS•	Grass and gravel tracks, grassy verge, field edge and some road walking
•LANDSCAPE•	Arable farmland, open meadow, airport runway and airport installations
•SUGGESTED MAP•	aqua3 OS Explorer 195 Braintree & Saffron Walden
•START / FINISH•	Grid reference: TL 528239
•DOG FRIENDLINESS•	Grassy verge next to airport perimeter fence is a great place for an off-lead sniff
•PARKING•	Informal street parking at Burton End village
•PUBLIC TOILETS•	None on route

BACKGROUND TO THE WALK

Stansted Airport is London's third international airport. Built on the site of an American airbase, its construction ended 50 years of debate as to where it should be sited. During the 1930s plans were announced for building an airport at Fairlop, near Hainault Forest, but these were overtaken by shortlists drawn up between the 1960s and 1970s for sites much further away from the urban fringe. One of these was Stansted and, after prolonged public debate, the airport opened in 1991.

One of the conditions of construction was that no soil was to be taken from the site, and as a result some interesting archaeological finds from neolithic to medieval times were discovered, some of which are displayed at Saffron Walden Museum. The striking design of the airport terminal, by Sir Norman Foster and much admired by visitors, is an example of how closely rural Essex is tied to the fortunes and changing needs of London.

The airport is one of the biggest employers in the area, currently employing 9,500, and is one of the fastest growing in England with modern terminal facilities. These include a spacious one-level terminal with natural light, minimum walking distances for passengers and state of the art equipment to monitor noise levels.

Going for a Burton

This walk starts at the tiny hamlet of Burton End, which is the nearest you'll get to the runway to see aircraft taking off and landing. Burton End with its attractive 18th- and 19th-century cottages and houses, like its neighbour, Tye Green with its pleasant green and thatched dwellings, seems untouched by the development of the airport and their proximity to the busy M11. As you traverse arable fields you can't fail to hear the roar of aircraft engines as they take off or come into land. In your meander across the beautiful rolling countryside of north west Essex you may be surprised to discover a railway track, a spur line from Stansted Mountfitchet, which disappears beneath the airport runway. This line is the

Stansted Express, which connects passengers with London's Liverpool Street Station and the airport terminal.

By far the most frequent visitors to the quiet lanes of Burton End and Tye Green are plane spotters who seem to come out in all weathers to pursue their hobby from the grassy verges skirting the airport perimeter fence. If you're into plane spotting, or spotting plane spotters, or just enjoy the countryside with rather surreal views of roaring metal-winged birds swooping from the skies, rather than the feathered kind that twitters and sings in tranquil woodland, then this walk may be right up your runway.

Walk 42 Directions

① Follow the fingerpost opposite the poultry farm at **Burton End** and walk between houses to the arable field. Ignore the fingerpost on the left and follow the field-edge path with the ditch and hedgerows to your right. At the waymark, cross between bushes and maintain direction half left with the ditch and hedgerow on your left.

② Maintain direction, turning right and left at the waymarks, until you reach the waymark on the edge of the copse of trees and the footbridge. Turn right and after 300yds (274m) take the footbridge

WHILE YOU'RE THERE ⓘ
Take an informal tour of **Stansted Airport** where you can indulge in retail therapy, enjoy a drink or meal, go to church, or sit back and dream about your next holiday. If you've had enough of tramping in muddy Essex fields you can even book a flight and take off for some blue-skied tropical paradise.

WHAT TO LOOK FOR ⓘ
The best place at Stansted for watching aircraft take off is on the mound beside the fire service training centre of Stansted Airport. To see them land keep to the embankment along the perimeter fence near Claypit Hill. In both locations you can join plane spotters, complete with 'poles' or telescopes, spotting Jumbo jets and a host of other multi-coloured aircraft emblazoned with serial numbers and their airlines name.

left over the railway cutting. This is the spur line to Stansted Airport so you can even plane and train spot at the same time. Once over the bridge, turn left with the railway on your left and, at the waymark, turn right on to the cross-field path to emerge at **Tye Green Road**.

③ Turn right on to Tye Green Road. At the houses, turn left to explore old cottages and the moated farm at **Tye Green**. Follow the track around **The Green** back to **Tye Green Road** and turn left along the road which changes its name to **Claypit Hill**. The road bears sharply right, opposite is the emergency gateway set in the perimeter fence of **Stansted Airport**. From here, if there is room, you can jostle for position with plane spotters to watch aircraft landing.

④ In front of the fence, turn right to walk along the verge between the airport perimeter fence and the road. Maintain your direction following the path around the

control tower and fire service training centre. At the grassy mound, possibly earthworks from the runway, there is some parking used by plane spotters.

⑤ Turn right on to the farm track between **Riders Farm** and **Monks Farm** to the three-way junction at **Belmer Road** and then turn left. Call in at the **Ash** public house on your left, although the tree after which it is named no longer exists. Here there is a large car park and garden area, popular at lunch time with aircraft maintenance workers from the nearby hangars. From the pub, turn left passing **Warmans Farm** on your right and return to your car at **Burton End**.

WHERE TO EAT AND DRINK ⓘ
Fodder is scarce along the perimeter fence so your best bet is to take your own. The only eaterie in the area is the attractive thatched-roof **Ash** pub at Burton End, which offers wholesome soups and warming curries amongst other goodies in winter. In the summer enjoy home-cooked meals al fresco in the delightful beer garden. Open all day.

On the Ground at Stansted

A suprisingly rural saunter around the ancient and modern sights of Stansted Mountfitchet.

•DISTANCE•	5¾ miles (9.2km)
•MINIMUM TIME•	2hrs 15min
•ASCENT / GRADIENT•	101ft (34m) ▲ ▲ ▲
•LEVEL OF DIFFICULTY•	🚶 🚶 🚶
•PATHS•	Grassy and forest tracks, field edge and some street walking
•LANDSCAPE•	Arable farmland, grazing meadow, some forest and motorway
•SUGGESTED MAP•	aqua3 OS Explorer 195 Braintree & Saffron Walden
•START / FINISH•	Grid reference: TL 515248
•DOG FRIENDLINESS•	On lead for most of way and a bit too noisy near M11
•PARKING•	Pay-and-display at Lower Street
•PUBLIC TOILETS•	Lower Street car park

BACKGROUND TO THE WALK

Some passengers flying in from the Continent bound for Stansted may be surprised to peer out of the window and spot a Norman castle on a hill, around which is a village, a brook and a railway line. On landing they may be even more surprised to learn that this castle is only 2 miles (3.2km) away at Stansted Mountfitchet. In this walk we take a trip back in time to the 11th century and explore the rural delights surrounding Stansted Montfitchet.

Stansted appears in the Domesday Book as Stansteda, a Saxon name meaning stony place. After the Norman conquest, William I granted the lordship of the manor to the Gernon family, who later changed their name to Montfitchet. The Montfitchet family came from Normandy and during the 12th century Richard de Montfitchet built a motte and bailey castle. The second Richard de Montfitchet was one of five Essex barons who forced King John to sign the Magna Carta, and in revenge the King destroyed the castle in 1215. All that remains are the mound and part of the stone wall, but today you can visit an imaginative reconstruction of the castle complete with Norman village and interpretative displays showing what life was like in Norman times.

This walk takes in the pretty windmill on a hill at the back of the village before cutting across Stansted Brook and the railway line to old Stansted. We take a pleasant footpath passing the Manor House, one of the original vicarages of the beautiful Norman church, St Mary the Virgin, that stands in the grounds of Stansted Hall. The church, another legacy of the Montfitchet family, contains the worn figure of a 14th-century cross-legged knight believed to be that of Richard de Montfitchet. Stansted Hall is now the Arthur Findlay College for Psychic Studies, colloquially known as 'Spook Hall'.

You're suddenly brought into the 21st century as you cross the bridge over the busy M11 and return to Stansted Mountfitchet via the delightful hamlet of Birchanger which is blessed with views of rolling countryside and woodlands. In Stansted Mountfitchet you can see old houses and pubs, some dating back to the 16th and 17th centuries and the village sign, depicting the Montfitchet shield, standing as a statement reminding visitors and locals that their heritage must be conserved.

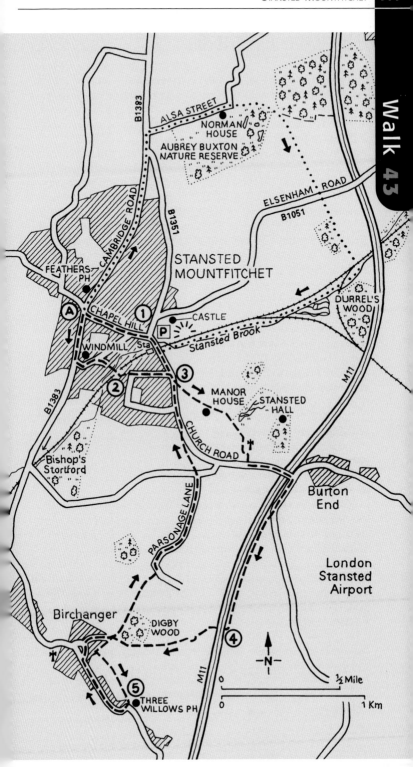

Walk 43 **Directions**

① From the car park turn left into **Lower Street** and cross into **Chapel Hill**. At the top of the hill turn left at the traffic lights on to the **B138** and take the next left into **Millside**. Pass the windmill on the left and turn right into **Brook Road** where after 100yds (91m) walk between houses to the footbridge over **Stansted Brook**.

② Cross Stansted Brook and turn left so that the brook is on your left. Take the slope up to the railway footbridge on your right to cross the line. Turn left and bear right uphill into **Park Road** through the housing estate to the T-junction. Here turn right into **Church Road** and, a few paces after Churchfields, bear left on to the concrete track signposted '**Manor House**'.

③ Maintain direction along the track keeping to the left of Manor House where it becomes a narrow path. Pass by the line of trees and an arable field to your left. Keep the church to your left and follow the path to **Church Road**. Turn left and after the gate for S**tansted Hall**, cross over the **M11** and at the T-junction turn right. After 250yds (229m) follow the fingerpost through the hedgerow on to the track running parallel with the M11. Maintain direction for 1,000yds (914m).

④ Turn right into the tunnel under the **M11**. Turn left along the field-edge path following the ditch. After 200yds (183m), turn left over the concrete slab bridge, left again on to the path and after a few paces turn right keeping the pond on your right. Follow the field-edge path for 100yds (91m), turn right over the second bridge, then left and right to maintain direction keeping the hedgerow on your right. After 200yds (183m), cross the wooden bridge and continue across the field to the waymark where you turn half right with woods on your right. At the next waymark left, follow the field-edge path. After 150yds (137m), turn left with backs of houses on your right and emerge into **Birchanger Lane** next to the **Three Willows** pub.

> **WHAT TO LOOK FOR** ⓘ
>
> Inside the **Norman church** at Birchanger look for the brass memorial depicting a solider and a machine gun. One of the few modern brasses in the country, it commemorates Jack Watney, a 19-year-old Birchanger boy, who died in the Boer War in 1901.

⑤ Turn right at Birchanger Lane and right into **Wood Lane**. Continue along the track, with Digby Wood on your right, to **Parsonage Lane**. Turn left along the road to cross **Foresthall Road** on to the footpath. After 300yds (274m) turn left into **Church Road** and return to the car park.

> **WHERE TO EAT AND DRINK** ⓘ
>
> There's just one pub in Birchanger, conveniently situated at the end of one of the footpaths. The 19th-century **Three Willows**, complete with pub sign depicting cricketer, W G Grace flanked by two batsmen, is both dog and child friendly and has a large grassy garden.

> **WHILE YOU'RE THERE** ⓘ
>
> **Stansted Windmill** at Stansted Mountfitchet was built in 1787 and donated to the village by Lord Blyth. It last worked in 1910 and if you're there on the first Sunday of the month from April to October or any Sunday in August between 2PM and 6PM you can go inside.

Stansted Mountfitchet

A different loop takes in wild places by a railway, nature reserve and castle.
See map and information panel for Walk 43

•**DISTANCE**•	4¾ miles (7.7km)
•**MINIMUM TIME**•	2hrs
•**ASCENT / GRADIENT**•	105ft (32m)
•**LEVEL OF DIFFICULTY**•	

Walk 44 Directions (Walk 43 option)

At the traffic lights on **Chapel Hill**, Point Ⓐ, turn right into the Cambridge road, an old Roman road, now the **B1383**, where a Victorian drinking fountain stands on the former site of the Cock Beer house. The Cambridge road used to be the old turnpike road along which there were several coaching inns. One of these, the **Feathers** on the left, dates back to the mid-19th century and is adjacent to some fine examples of 17th- and 18th-century pargetted and thatched buildings, evidence of a much older village which existed long before the airport.

After 1 mile (1.6km), turn right into **Alsa Street** passing the converted barns, which form the Business Park on your right. This is followed by the high wall of the imposing 18th-century **Norman House**. As the road bears sharp left, go straight ahead on to the bridleway and after 100yds (91m) you reach the entrance to the **Aubrey Buxton Nature Reserve**, Point Ⓑ. Originally the pleasure park to Norman House, this lovely woodland with six ponds was donated by Lady Buxton in 1976, and is managed by the Essex Wildlife Trust.

From the nature reserve, turn right along the bridleway passing **Keepers Cottage**. At the fingerpost, turn right and follow the bridleway downhill to **Elsenham Road**. Cross the road with care.

Follow the footpath past farm buildings downhill and into a tunnel under the London-to-Cambridge railway. Although surrounded by a triangle of road and rail bustle, formed by two railtracks and a motorway, this area is full of wildlife provided by the juxtaposition of **Durrell's Wood** and **Stansted Brook**. Turn right and pass through another two tunnels and maintain direction with the railway on your right and Stansted Brook on your left.

The path here may be narrow and very muddy after heavy rain. But you are surrounded by thick gorse, baby oak, reeds, sedges and the ubiquitous thistle which provide a wonderful habitat for all manner of insects. At the end of the footpath metal steps ascend beside a white timbered house to the bridge on **Church Road**. Turn right for views of the castle and rejoin Walk 43.

Walk 45

A Roam Around Roding Valley Nature Reserve

A wildlife wander on the former site of RAF Chigwell.

•DISTANCE•	3 miles (4.8km)
•MINIMUM TIME•	1hr 30min
•ASCENT / GRADIENT•	Negligible
•LEVEL OF DIFFICULTY•	
•PATHS•	Wide byways, tracks and sections of road
•LANDSCAPE•	River bank, open meadows and some urban views
•SUGGESTED MAP•	aqua3 OS Explorer 174 Epping Forest & Lee Valley
•START / FINISH•	Grid reference: TQ 428943
•DOG FRIENDLINESS•	Positively dog friendly, no stiles and off lead
•PARKING•	Small free car park by David Lloyd Centre off Roding Lane
•PUBLIC TOILETS•	None on route

Walk 45 Directions

Roding Valley Meadows Nature Reserve is situated on traditionally managed hay meadows which, from 1938 to 1968, were occupied by RAF Chigwell. Over 3,000 people lived and worked here in over 100 buildings, which included hangars, a theatre, a post office and a shop. Now demolished, it's hard to believe that this nature reserve with its peaceful paths and meadows was once home to such a community.

From the **information board** at the entrance go through the kissing gate where there are two paths. The one straight ahead is wide and gravelly, but to start the walk take the path on the right to the steep embankment. This narrow hillside was created from earth dug out during the construction of the M11. This path is seldom used and has become an excellent hunting ground for kestrels and sparrow hawks. Also from here you can look

down on the recreation area and the lake which, although not part of the reserve, is a popular spot for many waterfowl. After exploring this area return to your starting point and take the main path into the reserve.

After 50yds (46m), a wooden footbridge spans the **River Roding** to the lake area in the recreation park. But, to follow the nature reserve, go straight ahead for about 200yds (183m) through oak and hornbeam and stop at the concrete area, site of RAF Chigwell. Continue along this concrete path, bearing right until the path ends at

---

WHAT TO LOOK FOR　　　ⓘ

Near the picnic area, look for the thick **iron rings** in the ground from which barrage balloons from RAF Chigwell were strung during World War Two. Near by is a flat stone, made by an airman from the unit, which reads, '1943 Intone.' This commemorates an operation involving a Mobile Signals Unit from RAF Chigwell, which went to the Azores to destroy German submarines.

> **WHERE TO EAT AND DRINK** ⓘ
> The Railway Tavern in Buckhurst Hill
> provides good pub grub in a homely
> setting or try the atmospheric Ye Olde
> Kings Head at Chigwell, immortalised by
> Charles Dickens in *Barnaby Rudge* and a
> one-time favourite haunt of personnel
> from RAF Chigwell. Alternatively pack a
> picnic and enjoy it at the reserve.

a small roundabout surrounded by open meadow. The seating here provides a good picnic area and a place to watch for skylarks nesting in the meadow ahead.

Now take the grassy path which leads away from the concrete roundabout. Red waymark signs direct you around the edge of **Four Acres Field** to the left and along the cross path, an ancient green lane which once formed part of the drovers' and packhorse route from Epping Forest to Romford market. Continue along this path towards the tall thin chimney which is a Victorian vent for underground sewers. Bear left into the grass area known as **Lower Mead** following the waymark. This is cut regularly for hay which, combined with winter grazing, is a traditional method of looking after grassland and encourages wild flowers to grow. In spring it is a riot of colour.

The path now continues with the **River Roding** to your right providing a habitat for kingfishers, dragonflies, damselflies, bream and sticklebacks. After 300yds (274m), cross the river on **Charlie Moule's footbridge**, built in the 1950s to replace stepping stones. Turn right on to the concrete path with the river on your right, and continue until you reach **waymark B** where you can see **Great Horsley Pond**. The pond, cleared every two years,

is a haven for dragonflies. Here the Great Horsley Fen, wet all year round, is surrounded by reeds and the rare brown sedge which thrive in these conditions.

Continue along the concrete path passing **waymarks C** and **D**. You can now see the houses of Loughton and Debden near by, incongruously close to this lovely reserve. Follow the path to the **River Roding** and turn right with the river on your left. This is another fine area to sit and maybe picnic or rest before continuing ahead to return to **Charlie Moule's footbridge**. Cross the bridge and continue through ancient meads, or meadows, with the river on your right. Lower Mead and Further River Mead are Sites of Special Scientific Interest (SSSIs) and home to very rare wild flowers and grasses. The path continues ahead through thick woodland and what is almost a tunnel of dense blackthorn. Emerging from the blackthorn, the path leads into an area known as **Luscious Mead**, which is prone to flooding when the River Roding bursts its banks. These occasional incidents are important for the survival of plants dependent on the nutrient-rich soil. Walk a little way off the path towards the river to admire the willow trees on the river bank.

Follow the path between hedges to secluded **Andrew's Pond**, home to grass snakes and water voles. This is a pleasant picnic spot and any crumbs you may drop will soon be swooped on by the birds in the surrounding trees. Walk anti-clockwise around the pond, following the **River Roding** on your right. At the footbridge turn left and return to the car park.

Epping Forest Retreat

Follow Queen Victoria's path to the opening of the forest to Londoners.

•DISTANCE•	7¼ miles (11.7km)
•MINIMUM TIME•	3hrs 30min
•ASCENT / GRADIENT•	227ft (70m) ▲▲▲
•LEVEL OF DIFFICULTY•	🚶🚶 🚶
•PATHS•	Woodland paths and bridleways, some road
•LANDSCAPE•	Ponds, ancient woodland and open heathland
•SUGGESTED MAP•	aqua3 OS Explorer 174 Epping Forest & Lee Valley
•START / FINISH•	Grid reference: TQ 404950
•DOG FRIENDLINESS•	Great fun, though a bit muddy. Keep on lead around horses
•PARKING•	Free car park on A1069 at Connaught Water
•PUBLIC TOILETS•	Epping Forest Conservation Centre

BACKGROUND TO THE WALK

Shaped like a crescent and extending 12 miles (19.3km) south from Epping to Wanstead Flats, Epping Forest is divided by the Epping New Road which gives access from north east London to the M25. But for all the traffic, you need step back only a little to discover tranquil tracks and pathways meandering through 6,000 acres (2,430ha) of ancient woodland. For Epping Forest is one of the few places where you can still see the effects of medieval forest management and today is a popular recreational retreat attracting all those yearning to escape city life.

A Gift from a Queen

You can follow Queen Victoria's route from Connaught Water, near Chingford Station where she arrived in 1882 to declare, 'It gives me the greatest satisfaction to dedicate this beautiful forest to the use and enjoyment of my people for all time'. She rode in an open carriage along Fairmead Bottom to High Beach to the cheers of the crowds of Cockneys, mostly hell-bent on having a good day out.

Prior to this, the forest was a hunting ground reserved for royals. Queen Elizabeth I used to hunt from the lodge named after her, now the Epping Forest Museum, and probably galloped over an early Roman settlement, Loughton Camp, a few miles to the east. Stray off pathways and into deep shaded glades and you might be lucky enough to spot fallow or mutjac deer, descendants of the dark fallow deer introduced by James I in 1612. You can also enjoy the gently rolling landscape near the Kings Oak pub where Henry VIII breakfasted on 19 May 1536 as he waited to hear the news that Anne Boleyn had been executed.

At the Epping Forest Conservation Centre, a trail leads you through an ancient landscape of coppiced and pollarded trees. In medieval times cattle and deer were free to graze and woodsmen harvested wood for domestic purposes, a practice which ceased in 1878. Trees were coppiced, or cut to ground level, allowing new shoots to grow from the stump, but if left unfenced made easy fodder for animals. To save the trees from further damage and to keep them out of the reach of peckish livestock, the branches were cut above head height every 12 to 15 years, a system known as pollarding. Explore the forest today and you'll find several thousand of these pollarded trees, identifiable by their massive crowns.

0 ½ Mile

0 1 Km

-N-

High Beach

105

Lippitts Hill

HIGH BEACH CHURCH

CENTENARY WALK

EPPING FOREST

WHITEHOUSE PLAIN

BURY WOOD

Sewardstonebury

ESSEX

GTR LONDON

QUEEN ELIZABETH'S HUNTING LODGE

BUTLERS RETREAT

Woodford

P ④ KINGS OAK PH

WC

PAUL'S NURSERY

EPPING FOREST CONSERVATION CENTRE

⑤ ③ A104

TEA HUT

P

⑥

NORTH LONG HILLS

FAIRMEAD POND

FAIRMEAD BOTTOM

Loughton

LONG HILLS

GREEN RIDE

② PALMER'S BRIDGE

EPPING NEW ROAD

A121

CONNAUGHT WATER

P

① A1069 A104

Earl's Path

Walk 46 Directions

① From the car park walk between wooden posts and bear left on the gravel path which hugs **Connaught Water**. Walk around the lake for 800yds (732m), turn left over the footbridge and along the path with high trees to **Fairmead Bottom**. This low-lying area may flood after heavy rain.

② After 400yds (366m), turn left on to the disused tarmac road and after a few paces cross **Palmer's Bridge** and bear right on to the grassy track, which continues ahead close to the A104 on your right. The path crosses meadows to **Fairmead Pond** on your left and after 750yds (686m), turn left on to the road uphill and into the car park where there is a tea hut.

③ Continue up the tarmac road for 100yds (91m) and turn right by the metal gate on to the wide hoggin bridleway, which undulates through high woods and pollarded beech trees. Maintain direction for ½ mile (800m) and take the path left, which leads into the wooden fenced enclosure of **Epping Forest Conservation Centre**.

④ Leave the Conservation Centre by the front path, turn left and walk past the **Kings Head** public house. After 300yds (274m), with **Paul's Nursery** on your left, take the path

right. Walk under high trees for 250yds (229m) to reach the tarmac road and the secluded location of **High Beech church.** With the church behind you, turn left downhill and after 300yds (274m), turn right on to the path between high pollarded trees.

⑤ This is the **Centenary Walk**, which maintains direction through thick woodland for ½ mile (800m) to the deep cutting of the small brook. Walk downhill south west, keeping the brook on your right and after 400yds (366m), at the wide grassy cross path, turn left.

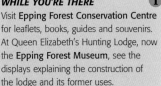

WHILE YOU'RE THERE
Visit **Epping Forest Conservation Centre** for leaflets, books, guides and souvenirs. At Queen Elizabeth's Hunting Lodge, now the **Epping Forest Museum**, see the displays explaining the construction of the lodge and its former uses.

⑥ After 300yds (274m), turn right on to the **Green Ride** bridleway. This popular horse ride bisects North Long Hills and White House Plain. At the confluence of paths maintain your direction through **Bury Wood** and at cross paths walk half right taking the uphill track. Ahead notice the wooden frame of Butlers Retreat, a popular watering hole next to the **Queen Elizabeth Hunting Lodge**. Turn left downhill by the **A1069** and return to the car park.

WHERE TO EAT AND DRINK
Butler's Retreat provides excellent snacks and meals. For pub fare try the **Kings Oak** or tuck into a salt beef sandwich at the adjacent snack bar. For hot drinks and a slice of fruit cake you can't go wrong at the green **tea huts** inside the forest.

WHAT TO LOOK FOR
There are over 50 species of tree including oak, hornbeam, beech and birch, pollarded and coppiced trees, near Kings Oak pub. Motor cycle *aficionados* might like the atmosphere and display of powerful machines with their leather-clad riders who gather near the tea hut on Sunday mornings.

A Scout Round Gilwell Park

A fairly challenging walk combining superb London views and the wooded parkland of the headquarters of the Scout Association.

•DISTANCE•	6 miles (9.7km)
•MINIMUM TIME•	2hrs 30min
•ASCENT / GRADIENT•	231ft (70m) ▲▲▲
•LEVEL OF DIFFICULTY•	🏃 🏃 🏃
•PATHS•	Grassy paths, forest tracks, green lanes, some stretches of road, 9 stiles
•LANDSCAPE•	Forest, park, reservoir, waterways and rolling countryside
•SUGGESTED MAP•	aqua3 OS Explorer 174 Epping Forest & Lee Valley
•START / FINISH•	Grid reference:TQ 387963
•DOG FRIENDLINESS•	Great open spaces and forest to sniff about in, but watch for horses and packs of cub scouts
•PARKING•	Free car park in Gilwell Lane
•PUBLIC TOILETS•	None on route

BACKGROUND TO THE WALK

Every scout has heard of Gilwell Park, the international training and camp centre for the Scout Association. Set on a plateau and flanked by King George's Reservoir in the west and Epping Forest in the east, the 108 acre (43.7ha) wooded estate was bought for the Scout Association in 1919 by a wealthy Scottish publisher, William F de Bois Maclaren.

Through the Estate

A public footpath passes through the estate giving views of the monuments, statues, camp fire circles, scout huts and in the distance, the White House, now Gilwell Park Hotel and Conference Centre, before descending towards the reservoir. The White House dates back to the 15th century but was nothing like the grand building you see today. In the mid-18th century it was rebuilt and over the years extended, and renamed, by various owners.

Perhaps the most dynamic occupants were William and Margaret Chinnery, who lived here from 1792 to 1812 and brought new life to the area. They were patrons of the arts, threw lavish parties and were seen in all the right places. But tragedy struck; two of their children died, one aged 12 and the other 21, and shortly afterwards William was dismissed from his Civil Service post when he was accused of fraud. He fled to Gothenburg and never returned. Margaret moved to Paris but never forgot the 'earthly paradise' that was Gilwell Hall.

Scouting for Boys

In 1858 William Alfred Gibbs, better known as the inventor of Gibbs Dentifrice toothpaste, became the new owner but he couldn't afford the upkeep of the house, which was in ruins by the time it was sold to the Scout Association for £7,000. In 1994 the White House was completely renovated but if you visit today take care; they say that some parts are haunted and that a female ghost walks late at night lamenting the loss of her children. Some have even heard strange rattling chains and clanking footsteps and others swear they have spotted the figure of Dick Turpin astride Black Bess.

Scouting round Gilwell Park involves some sharp climbs and slippery descents especially after rain, but the views of north London from the top of Barn Hill are well worth the effort. This walk also takes in the forest paths around Lippitts Hill where you may hear close range gunfire and helicopters hovering above a set of army-like buildings. You could be forgiven for thinking that you have accidentally strayed in to an SAS training camp but the truth is that you are adjacent to the firearms training camp and helicopter base of the Metropolitan Police. Lord Baden-Powell of Gilwell, founder of the Scout Movement, no doubt would have warned his protégés to watch out and, if anything, to 'Be Prepared.'

Walk 47 **Directions**

① From the car park turn right and pass through the gates of **Gilwell Park** following the yellow waymark. Keep to the wide grassy path between trees and the Scout Association buildings. At the top of the hill there are panoramic views of the reservoir. Follow the steep downhill path with the wood and the pond on your right and go over the stile to emerge beside the village hall at **Sewardstone**.

② Turn left into **Dawes Hill** and left again into **Sewardstone Road**. Turn right into **Mill Lane** passing houses and maintain your direction on the downhill track towards **King**

George's Reservoir. Turn right and follow the track, with the reservoir and **Horsemill Stream** on your left, to the footbridge over the stream.

③ Do not cross the bridge. Go straight through the kissing gate and turn right on to the waymarked **London Loop** path, walking east to **Sewardstone Road**. Turn right and after 100yds (91m), turn left over the stile and ignore the **London Loop** path right. Walk up the steep north flank of **Barn Hill**, stopping to look around occasionally at tremendous views over reservoirs, Epping Forest and Waltham Abbey.

④ After crossing the gravel path and the seventh stile, turn right on to the wide **Green Lane**. Maintain direction and turn left at the second fingerpost marked 'Lippitts Hill'. Bear left past the police firearms training camp fence on your right and don't be alarmed if it sounds as though there's a war going on. The marksmen are well away from you.

⑤ At **Lippitts Hill**, turn right passing the training camp and the **Owl** pub, the gardens of which afford lovely views across Epping Forest. Fifty yards (46m) after the pub turn right at the fingerpost, go up wooden steps and on to the steep grassy downhill path. Maintain your

> **WHILE YOU'RE THERE** ⓘ
> Depending on the weather and availability of staff you may be able to join a guided tour of **Gilwell Park**, which includes the campsite, the White House and the training centre. Visitors should report to the Warden in Camp Square or telephone 0208 498 5300 in advance. You can also buy a range of booklets, souvenirs and maps from the shop on the site.

direction between horse paddocks and cross the stile, followed by the footbridge and another stile. Follow the path over undulating meadow across the flank of the hill, then downhill to houses on your left. At the double fingerpost, ignore the direction to **Hornbeam Lane**, but turn right to **Sewardstonebury**, following the line of oak trees across **West Essex Golf Course**. Maintain direction across fairways and past houses to emerge into **Bury Road**. Turn right and then first left to return to the car park.

> **WHAT TO LOOK FOR** ⓘ
> **Big Mac**, nothing to do with a hamburger, is a clock tower in Camp Square named after camp warden, Alfred Macintosh, who advocated that a clock should be placed high enough so that it could be seen right across the main camping field of Gilwell Park. Scouts from Bermondsey raised the cash for Big Mac, which is clearly visible from the footpath at the start of the walk.

> **WHERE TO EAT AND DRINK** ⓘ
> The 18th-century **White House** is a conference and training centre for the Scout Association but also doubles as a hotel with a very pleasant restaurant. Combine lunch with an informal tour of the public rooms, which are decorated with scouting memorabilia and paintings, including one used on the set of ITV's *Coronation Street*. Pub grub can be had at the **Owl** at Lippitts Hill opposite the police firearms training camp.

Walk 48

Lee Valley Park

An adventurous and challenging walk following the 'gunpowder plot' at Waltham Abbey, waterways, ancient woodlands and a host of views.

•DISTANCE•	7½ miles (12.1km)
•MINIMUM TIME•	4hrs 30min
•ASCENT / GRADIENT•	269ft (82m) ▲▲▲
•LEVEL OF DIFFICULTY•	🚶 🚶 🚶
•PATHS•	Grassy riverside, steep field paths, green lanes prone to mud after rain, short stretch of road, 5 stiles
•LANDSCAPE•	Country park, woodland, waterways and marshes
•SUGGESTED MAP•	aqua3 OS Explorer 174 Epping Forest & Lee Valley
•START / FINISH•	Grid reference: TL 384015
•DOG FRIENDLINESS•	A lot of time on lead for such a big space. Waltham Road unpleasant
•PARKING•	Free car park at Cornmill Meadows, closes at 6PM
•PUBLIC TOILETS•	Near the Bittern Watchpoint at Fishers Green

BACKGROUND TO THE WALK

You could spend an entire day doing nothing more strenuous than enjoying the recreational facilities of the Lee Valley Country Park. The 1,000 acres (405ha) on either side of the River Lee between Waltham Abbey in Essex and Broxbourne in Hertfordshire consist of lakes, waterways, open space and countryside linked by paths, walkways and cycle tracks. But this walk, admittedly challenging, takes you along river paths and bridleways, which explore the edge of an ancient forest rewarding you with fine panoramic views of London.

The Royal Gunpowder Mills

On your meanderings through Lee Valley you might mention the gunpowder plot to the residents of Waltham Abbey and they may well return a quizzical look. Guy Fawkes might have procured some gunpowder hereabouts, but the only plot is a rather large one consisting of 175 acres (71ha) of parkland complete with 21 buildings and now a tourist attraction offering guided tours. Known as the Royal Gunpowder Mills, it combines history and science to produce an explosive cocktail, sure to delight all ages.

This walk takes you along the perimeter of the former 300-year-old gunpowder factory, where safety was paramount in the handling of explosives. Cut off from the urbanisation and development of the surrounding area, it became a wildlife haven and today boasts the biggest heronry in Essex. You will pass alder woods where trees once produced charcoal for gunpowder manufacture while in Galleyhill Wood, part of Epping Forest, you'll discover coppiced and pollarded trees, an ancient form of forest management still in use today, which allows plant and insect life to proliferate on the forest floor.

Local Employer

Gunpowder was first manufactured here in the 1600s. In 1735 John Walton bought the Gunpowder Mill and his family churned out the stuff for the next 120 years. It was bought by the Crown in 1787 and became particularly handy during the Napoleonic Wars when production soared from 5,000 to 25,000 barrels a year. The factory sprawled across the Lee Valley and was connected by a complex network of canals to the Lee Valley Navigation and later by a narrow guage railway to the arsenal and ammunition factory at Enfield. It also provided employment for many local women during the World War One before closing its doors to become an explosives research and development establishment.

Walk 48 Directions

① From the rear of the car park at Cornmill Meadows, take the gravel path to the fingerpost and go straight ahead through woodland.

At **Cornmill Stream** turn right with the stream down on your left-hand side and views across Cornmill Meadow. At the footbridge turn right following the perimeter fence of the Waltham Abbey **Royal Gunpowder Mills**.

Walk 48

② Keep the fence on your left until reaching the cross-field path towards alder woodland. Follow the field-edge path with the brook on your left, signposted '**Hook Marsh**'. Turn left on to **Fishers Green Lane**, which leads to the car park and information board.

③ Cross two footbridges over the streams and go through the kissing gate on the right signposted 'Ware'. Follow the gravel path and picnic area bounded by **Seventy Acres Lake** on the left.

④ After 600yds (549m) at the fingerpost indicating '**Lea Valley Park farms and Nazeing**', cross the footbridge and turn left passing the Bittern Watchpoint. After crossing the access road to the electricity sub-station, follow the riverside path until you emerge at the tarmac road. Turn right and then left through the kissing gate and maintain direction. On your left is a birdwatching stand overlooking the marshes.

⑤ Proceed to the entrance of the sailing club. Here cross two stiles on your right and walk along the field-edge path keeping the sailing club on your left. Keep to the path as it bears right uphill to another stile.

WHILE YOU'RE THERE ⓘ
Visit the Royal Gunpowder Mills at Waltham Abbey for an explosive day out. You can create your own explosion through interactive computer displays, find out what it was like to work here or join a guided tour which includes wildlife watching from the tower and a visit to the largest heronry in Essex. This is one of the most important sites in Europe for the history of explosives and its recently renovated site is a must-see for those interested in industrial archaeology.

WHERE TO EAT AND DRINK ⓘ
The Coach & Horses on the corner of St Leonard's Road makes a welcome stop for a pie and a pint. It's conveniently situated mid-way through this walk and if you sit at the outdoor tables you have fine views of Galleyhill Wood on the hill. Alternatively stock up on goodies and enjoy the waterside views at the picnic area at Seventy Acres Lake.

⑥ At the top of the hill look back for wonderful views of north London and Hertfordshire. Follow the fingerpost for **Clayton Hill** through the kissing gate, cross the wooden bridge and emerge at **Coleman's Shaw**. Turn right on to the **B194** and follow the road as it goes downhill.

⑦ At the T-junction, turn left at the **Coach & Horses** pub into **Waltham Road**. Cross carefully and walk uphill past **Denver Lodge Farm** on the right. Cross the stile on the right and follow the field-edge path to **Galleyhill Wood**. Cross the next stile and continue, keeping the woods on your right, to the break in the trees. Walk through and at the cross path turn right on to the green lane to **Aimes Green**. At Aimes Green, turn right and after 100yds (91m), turn left in front of houses to join **Claygate Lane** to emerge beside **Eagle Lodge**. Cross **Crooked Mile Road** to the meadow and turn left through the kissing gate and return to the car park.

WHAT TO LOOK FOR ⓘ
If it's a clear day and you're feeling adventurous and don't mind scrambling up the embankment of Claygate Lane Track on your way back to Cornmill Meadows car park you can treat yourself to some far-reaching views of London, including Canary Wharf and the television masts of Alexandra Palace.

Waltham Abbey

Modern monuments, dragonfly-filled streams and an ancient abbey.
See map and information panel for Walk 48

Walk 49

•DISTANCE•	9 miles (14.5km)
•MINIMUM TIME•	5hrs 30min
•ASCENT / GRADIENT•	269ft (82m) ▲▲▲
•LEVEL OF DIFFICULTY•	🚶 🚶 🚶

Walk 49 Directions (Walk 48 option)

For a different start to Walk 48 at the car park, Point Ⓐ, turn left at the fingerpost marked Lee Valley and walk through the arboretum where trees were grown to supply London parks. After ½ mile (800m), cross two wooden footbridges over the tributaries of **Cornmill Stream**. Ignore the B194 ahead, turn right across meadow and after 150yds (137m) on your left is the modern **Discovery monument**, on the Greenwich Meridian Line.

Cross the metal footbridge over Cornmill Stream to the **Dragonfly Sanctuary and Abbey Fishponds**. Turn left under the **B194** to emerge on the grassy path leading to another bridge over Cornmill Stream. On your left are the remains of Harold Bridge which provided access for carts to the abbey farmyard. You now have fine views of the church of Waltham Abbey to your right.

Founded in Saxon times as a college, in 1066 it became the burial place of King Harold. Henry II established an Augustinian priory here, as penance for Thomas Becket's murder. It was raised to abbey status in 1184 and was the last to be dissolved by Henry VIII. All that remains of the abbey is the Great West Tower and nave, now Waltham Abbey church.

Pass the visitors' centre on your left and follow the path through the coaching entrance of the **Welsh Harp** pub into **Market Place**. Turn left into **Sun Street** and left again after the **Angel** pub passing the rear of shops to the break in the abbey walls. Here follow the fingerpost back to the Dragonfly Sanctuary, keeping the stream on your right for ½ mile (800m). Cross the bridge and turn left to join Walk 48 at Point ② or turn right to return to the car park, making this a 2¼ mile (3.6km) walk.

Theydon Bois to the End of the Line

A linear walk overground to the underground crossing the M25 tunnel.

•DISTANCE•	4 miles (6.4km)
•MINIMUM TIME•	1hr 30min
•ASCENT / GRADIENT•	217ft (65m) ▲▲▲
•LEVEL OF DIFFICULTY•	🏃 🏃 🏃
•PATHS•	Forest and grassy tracks, some urban streets
•LANDSCAPE•	Undulating ancient forestland, common and town views
•SUGGESTED MAP•	aqua3 OS Explorer 174 Epping Forest & Lee Valley
•START•	Grid reference: TQ 465990
•FINISH•	Grid reference: TL462016
•DOG FRIENDLINESS•	Dog-friendly woodlands and welcoming watering holes, can be off lead in forest
•PARKING•	Pay-and-display at Theydon Bois and Epping underground stations. Free off-street parking by The Green, Theydon Bois
•PUBLIC TOILETS•	Theydon Bois and Epping underground stations

Walk 50 Directions

Many parts of Epping Forest are well used, yet as the largest open space in the vicinity of London and Essex it is still possible to find tranquil niches even during the height of summer. One of these areas is in the northern reaches of the forest at Theydon Bois, where you don't even need your car to get there, as the area is well served by the underground. This walk takes you through the forest to emerge at the little town of Epping. Just 17 miles (27.4km) north east of London and at the end of the Central Line.

Turn left outside **Theydon Bois underground station**, passing the Railway Arms, into **Coppice Row**. Turn right and walk uphill passing **The Green** on your left and the Queen Victoria pub on your right.

Cross **Piercing Hill** and soon afterwards you pass the Theydon Bois schoolhouse, built in 1840, followed by St Mary's parish church with its delightful porch inscribed, 'There is no death'. Pause a moment here to admire the oak tree and the war memorial in the graveyard.

Coppice Row changes its name to become **Jack's Hill**, named after Jack Rann, a most notorious highwayman who robbed anything that moved. He was nicknamed

> **WHAT TO LOOK FOR**
>
> **Epping High Street** is a Conservation Area with many listed buildings dating back to the 18th century. Some of the oldest are an attractive group of 17th- and 18th-century cottages at Nos 98 to 110. Look for the plaque on the weather-boarded Co-op building, once the site of much electioneering by Sir Winston Churchill (1874–1965), before he became Prime Minister.

Walk 50

'Sixteen String Jack', because he appeared at the Old Bailey with 'sixteen coloured ribbons streaming from the knees of his breeches'. In Jack's Hill, the Sixteen String Jack pub, complete with inn sign, shows the grinning rogue preparing to meet his death at the gallows.

After the church, walk 200yds (183m) and turn right. Follow the path left through the forest, now walking uphill parallel with Jack's Hill. In amongst the trees and ditches you can picture a posse of highwaymen plotting their next robbery as stage coaches would speed their way along the main London road to and from Aldgate.

Continue uphill with the **B172** a few paces away on your left. At the cross path, with the car park on your left, go straight on, and at the next car park turn right on to the path known as the **Centenary Ride**. This is the Green Ride bridleway from Epping to Loughton. Keep to the main path, which is bounded by coppiced oak and hornbeams, many with gnarled trunks and grotesque shapes, which all add to the sinister atmosphere of the area.

The path dips after ½ mile (800m), where to the left through woodland is a sign indicating the Iron Age earthworks at **Amresbury Banks**. Legend has it that Queen Boudica fought her last battle against the Romans here but there is little evidence to support this story. Continue along the main forest path and you will see evidence of the 1987 storm damage, during which many trees were brought down. At the end of the ride, take the path half right across grassland to **Theydon Road**. Turn left with Ivy Chimneys Road on your right and walk towards **Bell Common**.

As you cross **Ivy Chimney Road**, look right and in the distance you can see vehicles on the M25 seemingly emerging from the ground beneath your feet. During the building of the busy M25 motorway in the 1980s, it was proposed to route the M25 over Bell Common. Fierce opposition from local citizens, forest lovers and the Conservators of Epping Forest resulted in a tunnel for the traffic, which has preserved the area we are walking on today.

Pass the **Forest Gate Inn** on your right and follow **Bell Common Road** with its attractive 18th-century cottages and houses, into **Epping**. Keep left on the grassy path across the common with the **High Road** close on your left. After crossing **Hemnall Street**, you will see the water tower, built in 1872, one of three tower landmarks which stand on a ridge of the main road and which can be seen for many miles around.

Continue along the attractive **High Street** with its weather-boarded cottages and shop fronts. Turn right beside the police station and right again into **Hartland Road**. Turn left into **Station Road** and downhill to **Epping underground station** – the end of the Central Line.

Walking in Safety

All these walks are suitable for any reasonably fit person, but less experienced walkers should try the easier walks first. Route finding is usually straightforward, but you will find that an Ordnance Survey map is a useful addition to the route maps and descriptions.

Risks

Although each walk here has been researched with a view to minimising the risks to the walkers who follow its route, no walk in the countryside can be considered to be completely free from risk. Walking in the outdoors will always require a degree of common sense and judgement to ensure that it is as safe as possible.

- Be particularly careful on cliff paths and in upland terrain, where the consequences of a slip can be very serious.

- Remember to check tidal conditions before walking on the seashore.

- Some sections of route are by, or cross, busy roads. Take care and remember traffic is a danger even on minor country lanes.

- Be careful around farmyard machinery and livestock, especially if you have children with you.

- Be aware of the consequences of changes in the weather and check the forecast before you set out. Carry spare clothing and a torch if you are walking in the winter months. Remember the weather can change very quickly at any time of the year, and in moorland and heathland areas, mist and fog can make route finding much harder. Don't set out in these conditions unless you are confident of your navigation skills in poor visibility. In summer remember to take account of the heat and sun; wear a hat and carry spare water.

- On walks away from centres of population you should carry a whistle and survival bag. If you do have an accident requiring the emergency services, make a note of your position as accurately as possible and dial 999.

Acknowledgements

The authors would like to thank Joan and Robert Brown for allowing their dog, Sadie, to accompany them on these walks and sniff out the finer points for dog walkers.

AA Publishing and Outcrop Publishing Services would like to thank Chartech for supplying aqua3 maps for this book. For more information visit their website: www.aqua3.com.

Series management: Outcrop Publishing Services Ltd, Cumbria
Series editor: Chris Bagshaw
Front cover: AA Photo Library/John Miller